W9-AYE-632

Children
of the
Kingdom

Children
of the
Kingdom

A Bahá'í Approach to Spiritual Parenting

By Daun E. Miller

Bahá'í
PUBLISHING

Wilmette, Illinois

Bahá'í Publishing
415 Linden Avenue, Wilmette, Illinois 60091-2844

Copyright © 2010 by the National Spiritual Assembly of the Bahá'ís of the United States

All rights reserved. Published 2010
Printed in the United States of America on acid-free paper ∞

13   12   11   10   4   3   2   1

Library of Congress Cataloging-in-Publication Data
Miller, Daun E.
  Children of the kingdom : a Baha'i approach to spiritual
parenting / by Daun E. Miller.
      p. cm.
  Includes bibliographical references.
  ISBN 978-1-931847-75-9 (pbk. : alk. paper) 1. Bahai
education of children. 2. Parenting—Religious aspects—Bahai
Faith. I. Title.
  BP388.E42M55 2010
  297.9'3441—dc22
                              2009050047

Permission has been obtained from the Bahá'í World Center for the inclusion of excerpts from *The Priceless Pearl* by Rúḥíyyih Rabbani.

Cover design by Nathan Miller
Book design by Patrick Falso

*To my wonderful husband, Rick, without whose love and support
this book would never have been written.*

*To my beloved sons, Aaron and Nathan, who continue to
inspire and to encourage me.*

And to all the beautiful souls who made such a difference in our lives.

CONTENTS

CONTENTS

CONTENTS

ACKNOWLEDGMENTS

My heartfelt thanks goes to:

Counselor Joan Lincoln for her kind and encouraging words.

Terry Cassiday for her willing support and advice.

Aaron and Jennifer Miller for their loving assistance in proof-reading and computer technology.

My wonderful readers—Rick Miller, Sarah Major, Michele Stearns, Denise Johnson, Leah Roberts, Ila DeVuyst, Liliya Zaydulina, Mariam Everett, Mark Perry, Amrollah Hemmat, Nathan Miller, Nina Retzlaff, and Carlos Quiroga-Lassépas—for their invaluable insights and suggestions.

And to songwriters and musicians Jim Seals and Dash Crofts, who gave voice to the dream.

LOVE

Know thou of a certainty that Love is the secret of God's
holy Dispensation, the manifestation of the All-Merciful,
the fountain of spiritual outpourings. Love is heaven's kindly light,
the Holy Spirit's eternal breath that vivifieth the human soul. . . .
Love is the light that guideth in darkness, the living link that uniteth
God with man, that assureth the progress of every illumined soul. . . .
Love revealeth with unfailing and limitless power
the mysteries latent in the universe.

—'Abdu'l-Bahá, Selections from the
Writings of 'Abdu'l-Bahá

PREFACE

Love is the beginning of all things. Without it, we could not speak of God or spiritual growth or spiritual parenting. It is the emphasis of this book. 'Abdu'l-Bahá tells us in his beautiful words, *"Love is heaven's kindly light."*[1] And children, for those of us who love them, are the light of our lives.

Twenty-five years ago, our first son was born. We named him "Aaron" after his great-grandfather. That day was the happiest day we had ever known. Later, we learned that his name meant "light" or "high mountain." That name fit him perfectly, for he was, indeed, a beautiful light from God. At that time, we had been Bahá'ís for only one year and were still in the process of learning about the Faith. And so we began the demanding and fascinating job of raising our child in a Faith that was new to us and with few Bahá'ís to guide us. I remember feeling overwhelmed at the thought of bringing up our child as a Bahá'í when I was not sure what a Bahá'í child should be. I knew I had the writings of Bahá'u'lláh and 'Abdu'l-Bahá to help me, though, and I knew I had a mother's love so strong that nothing could stop my attempt to educate my children spiritually, even if I could only faintly glimpse what that could possibly mean at the time.

I write this book for parents who are experiencing these same emotions and who have the same desire to give their children the very best of spiritual training. This goal is attainable—to educate our children not only to become good people and good citizens but, ultimately, to become spiritual beings whose personal strength and character are a direct result of their knowledge and love of God. In times like these, when life is difficult and the future is uncertain, we can give our children what we may have never had ourselves when we were young—the knowledge that we are here for a reason, and that reason is to know and to love God. We are so fortunate, at this time in the history of the world, to have the guidance found in the Bahá'í writings to assist us in this endeavor. By studying and reflecting upon the words of Bahá'u'lláh and of 'Abdu'l-Bahá, we gain a better understanding of what it means to be spiritual parents and a greater appreciation for the opportunity and the honor that God has given us of raising spiritual children.

The gift of parenting is a gift beyond measure. It is also a great responsibility. The time when children are young goes by very quickly, even though we may not realize it at the time. It does not seem that long ago that our second son was born. We named him "Nathan," meaning "gift of God," and he truly was a gift from God. That day, also, was the happiest day we had ever known. Our dream for our sons was that they would grow up as "children of the kingdom" in a world free of hatred, prejudice, and war. There were many of us who became Bahá'ís at that time who felt the same way. Unfortunately, the world has yet to become the place we had hoped it would be. Still, we have not lost our dreams, even though the way has been long and, at times, hard. It is because we see in our children, who are now the ages we were then, a light so bright it dispels the darkness in the world, it breathes of possibilities for the future, and it shines with rays of hope. It was all worth it, we have found—all our heartfelt efforts, all our groping in the dark, and all our faith that God would help us with these children. And He did. We are ever so grateful for the blessing.

INTRODUCTION:
A BRIEF HISTORY OF THE
BAHÁ'Í FAITH

In the middle of the nineteenth century in the land of Persia (what is now present-day Iran), a wonderful event took place. A new Messenger of God appeared, and His name was the Báb. The Báb, who was born Siyyid 'Alí-Muḥammad, announced that He was the Forerunner or "Gate" through which an even greater Messenger would come. He suffered great persecution and ultimately death because of this teaching, but His mission was to tell the world about Bahá'u'lláh.

Bahá'u'lláh, whose name means "the Glory of God," was born in 1817 in Persia to a family of noble lineage. He lived a life of privilege, but, as a young man, chose to renounce that lifestyle, along with a position in the court of the <u>sh</u>áh, and instead dedicate His life to serving the poor. As soon as Bahá'u'lláh learned of the Báb, He immediately recognized the Báb's high spiritual station and began to follow His teachings. Along with Bahá'u'lláh, thousands of people began to accept the Báb's message that the time had arrived for a new Messenger of God to appear.

The Báb and His followers were seen as serious threats to Islam by the Muslim clergy, and many Bábís were persecuted, imprisoned, and put to death for their beliefs. Bahá'u'lláh was also arrested and put in prison, and it was while He was confined in the dark dungeon of the Síyáh-Chál that He received a revelation from God. A few years later, after being released from prison and exiled to distant lands, He started teaching a new message, one of love for God, love for His Messengers, and love for all humanity.

One of the most important teachings that Bahá'u'lláh revealed was the unity of all religions. He taught that God has sent Messengers throughout time to teach His people how to worship Him, how to live together, and how to love one another. These Messengers, or "Manifestations of God" as they are often referred to in the Bahá'í writings, are sent by God in a progressive order so that humanity can learn the spiritual truths that are necessary at every stage of human history. Since God is the Unknowable, the All-Wise, these Manifestations also "manifest" the attributes of God so that humanity can learn how to live as spiritual beings.

The names of these Manifestations of God appear in the great religions of the world. They are Abraham, Moses, Zoroaster, Buddha, Krishna, Jesus, and Muḥammad. In this new Day (or new religious dispensation), God has sent us the Báb and Bahá'u'lláh. Although the history of the Bahá'í Faith is beyond the scope of this book, the writings of Bahá'u'lláh, Prophet-Founder of the Bahá'í Faith, are the spiritual foundation upon which this book is written. Bahá'ís believe that the writings of Bahá'u'lláh are the revealed Word of God.

During His lifetime, Bahá'u'lláh wrote many works of spiritual guidance and wisdom. One of these works was the Hidden Words, and another was the Kitáb-i-Aqdas, which means Most Holy Book. He also wrote epistles to the kings and rulers of the world, sharing with them this new message and warning them of what would befall them if they continued on their path of turning away from God and ignoring the needs of the people. Because Bahá'u'lláh claimed a new revelation from God, He was exiled from place to place until He came to the prison city of 'Akká across the bay from Haifa in what is now modern-day Israel. It was during this time that He chose Haifa to be the administrative center of His Faith.

After the ascension of Bahá'u'lláh in 1892, His son, 'Abdu'l-Bahá, whose name means "Servant of the Glory," was appointed head of the Bahá'í Faith and the authorized interpreter of Bahá'u'lláh's writings. Bahá'ís consider 'Abdu'l-Bahá to be a true Bahá'í and to be the perfect example to which we should all aspire. 'Abdu'l-Bahá wrote many tablets during his lifetime on a wide variety of subjects, some of which were commentaries on the spiritual education of children. The writings of 'Abdu'l-Bahá, along with the writings of Bahá'u'lláh and the Báb, constitute the sacred scriptures of the Bahá'í Faith.

When 'Abdu'l-Bahá died in 1921, his grandson Shoghi Effendi was appointed Guardian of the Bahá'í Faith. Shoghi Effendi designed the beautiful gardens around the Bahá'í shrines in Haifa and 'Akka, Israel, and led the development of the Faith throughout the world. He also designated certain individuals who had given significant service to the Faith as Hands of the Cause of God. It was these Hands of the Cause who directed the Faith after the passing of Shoghi Effendi in 1957. In 1963 the members of the Universal House of Justice were elected. These nine members were chosen from among the Bahá'ís of the world and their task was, and still is, to lead and to guide the Bahá'í world community.

There are many books that tell the story of the Bahá'í Faith and that recount its unique and powerful history. In this book, a few of these stories are told. It is hoped that this brief account of the history of the Faith will help readers gain a better understanding of the Bahá'í writings and a greater appreciation for the sources from which these wonderful quotes on the spiritual education of children have been taken.

1

THE BAHÁ'Í WRITINGS: A DOORWAY TO KNOWLEDGE

The beginning of all things is the knowledge of God. . . .

—*Bahá'u'lláh,* Gleanings from the
Writings of Bahá'u'lláh

In the Bahá'í writings we witness something new to the world—an emphasis on the spiritual education of children in the sacred texts of a world religion. Although the method of spiritual education in the Bahá'í Faith, at this time, is similar to that of other religions, the teachings of the Faith present a unique viewpoint, a glimpse of something greater, more spiritual, and more wonderful than we have ever known. We discover in the Bahá'í writings the person who we have the capacity to become—a higher, nobler, and more compassionate person than has ever existed before, a person who views the inhabitants of the world as one family.

This book is about our journey through the doorway that leads us to the knowledge of God. It is about my own discovery of the writings as I tried to apply them to my own children. Bahá'u'lláh states, *"Every word that proceedeth out of the mouth of God is endowed with such potency as can instill new life into every human frame, if ye be of them that comprehend this truth."*[1] It is my belief that it is never too late to instill new life in our children by sharing with them the beauty of the writings or by encouraging them to adopt spiritual principles and behaviors.

In the Bahá'í writings we encounter wisdom in simplicity and beauty in each carefully chosen word. Even when the meanings seem simple or somewhat obvious, it is quite another matter to put these teachings into practice, to make them a reality in the life of a child, or to appreciate their spiritual complexity. It is an endeavor that requires both courage and love. What I hope to accomplish with this book is to inspire you to fall in love with the writings, as I did so long ago, and impart this love to your children.

I have arranged these quotes in what I believe to be chronological order from pregnancy through adolescence so that busy parents can find what they need quickly and easily. Although many of the quotes apply to different age groups, I believe that particular quotes dealing with specific topics are crucial for parents to concentrate on when their children reach a certain age. Spiritual principles taught at the right ages achieve the greatest possible effects. Each chapter of the book, therefore, is built upon the previous one. It is my hope that parents will find helpful quotes and suggestions in every chapter, even if they read the book when their children are older.

I do not pretend to know all the secrets of spiritual parenting. Surely, as each generation progresses, we will witness a flowering of spiritual insights that will influence the way that we educate our children. Now, I can only share what I have gleaned from my own experience as a parent and from my own study of the writings. It is for all parents to study the writings for themselves, to try to figure out what the words are trying to say, and to find new ways to apply them to their own children.

We begin the process of spiritual parenting by focusing on the task at hand. 'Abdu'l-Bahá encourages us with these gentle words. He states, *"Knowledge is love. Study, listen to exhortations, think, try to understand the wisdom and greatness of God. The soil must be fertilized before the seed can be sown."*[2] As we walk through this doorway and discover our role as spiritual parents, we understand that we are not alone. We all travel this road together. We all listen for the voice of God. May you find your questions answered, your hearts comforted, and your souls uplifted by studying these heavenly words.

A poem by Howard Colby Ives

'Tis not from sages, nor from learned books
That man gains wisdom. In his secret breast
A Chamber lies wherein he sometimes looks
And listens. There his troubled soul finds rest,
And there, if he adores, his life is blest.

The gloomy dust which rises from men's minds,
In their eternal search for certainty,
Obscures the spirit's vision, and so blinds
The eye of heart that, failing Truth to see,
They grope and wander in perplexity.

But sometimes—Ah, that blessed, unwarned hour!
The dust is scattered by a mystic breeze:
Upon man's heated mind there falls a shower
From Fount Celestial, and his heart finds ease
Which only God can give—Such hours are these.[3]

2

THE INDIVIDUAL AS
SPIRITUAL BEING

O Son of Man! Veiled in My immemorial being and in the ancient eternity of My essence, I knew My love for thee; therefore I created thee, have engraved on thee Mine image and revealed to thee My beauty.

—*Bahá'u'lláh*, Hidden Words

It seems appropriate that we begin the topic of spiritual parenting with the recognition of ourselves as spiritual beings. In Bahá'u'lláh's treasured words, we learn the reason why we were created. God, like a loving parent, created us because He loves us. By studying these holy writings, we begin to understand our true nature as children of God and to become aware of our great potential for spiritual growth. We are given clues to this potential from numerous tablets revealed by Bahá'u'lláh concerning the soul and our spiritual destiny. How are we created in the image of God and in what ways has God revealed His beauty to us? Many questions, such as these, come to mind as we reflect upon these passages.

In the Bahá'í writings we encounter each human being as a unique creation of God, especially when compared to all other forms of life. Bahá'u'lláh states, *"Upon the inmost reality of each and every created thing He hath shed the light of one of His names, and made it a recipient of the glory of one of His attributes. Upon the reality of man, however, He hath focused the radiance of all of His names and attributes, and made it a mirror of His own Self."* [1] Why has God focused the radiance of all of His names and attributes upon the reality of humanity? Is it somehow connected to the great *love* He has for His children? And how can we, as mere human beings, possibly become so radiant as to mirror forth the attributes of God? These are questions that require time for reflection and meditation in order to comprehend the magnitude of the unique gift of life that God has given us.

It is this awareness that brings to our parenting the necessary vision for what our children can become, as well as the possibilities that lie hidden within us all. We do not need to know or fully understand all of these truths in order to begin the process of educating our children spiritually. We must, however, have an appreciation for the beauty and the mystery of the vision God has given us concerning our own spiritual reality, along with the faith that God will provide the guidance we need in order to make the right decisions for our family and for ourselves.

In a difficult world, it is not easy to be good parents. We should not forget to love ourselves as God's creation or to be patient with our spiritual progress. If we are to see the face of God in every person, then surely we should try to see it in our children and in ourselves as well. We sometimes worry that we might fall short of displaying those same attributes and attitudes that we try so hard to instill in our children. How are we to educate them when we are so new at learning these spiritual truths for ourselves? How do we change ourselves to become the people God wants us to be? Howard Colby Ives, a Unitarian minister who was going through a period of great spiritual turmoil and reflection, sought answers to these questions from 'Abdu'l-Bahá in 1912. Ives writes, "Under the influence of such tremendous thoughts as these I one day asked 'Abdu'l-Bahá how it could ever be possible for me, deep in the mass of weak and selfish humanity, ever to hope to attain when the goal was so high and great. He said that it is to be accomplished little by little; little by little. And I thought to myself, I have all eternity for this journey from self to God. The thing to do is to get started."[2]

Just as we begin the process of educating our children spiritually, so we continue the process of educating ourselves. The act of studying the writings in order to become better parents, along with instructing our children in the ways of God, will awaken the desire in our own souls for spiritual growth. As we teach our little ones their first prayers and sing to them the beautiful lullabies of the spirit, we impart God's words to our own yearning and childlike hearts. Most teachers know that the more they teach, the more they learn themselves. We all have much to learn.

The more we learn about the process of spiritual growth, the more we appreciate the bounty of this guidance from God. It is like a gift from a father to his beloved children. 'Abdu'l-Bahá helps us to appreciate how wonderful a gift it is when he writes,

From amongst all mankind hath He chosen you, and your eyes have been opened to the light of guidance and your ears attuned to

the music of the Company above; and blessed by abounding grace, your hearts and souls have been born into new life. Thank ye and praise ye God that the hand of infinite bestowals hath set upon your heads this gem-studded crown, this crown whose lustrous jewels will forever flash and sparkle down all the reaches of time.

To thank Him for this, make ye a mighty effort, and choose for yourselves a noble goal. . . . Thus may each one of you be even as a candle casting its light, the center of attraction wherever people come together; and from you, as from a bed of flowers, may sweet scents be shed.[3]

3

MARRIAGE AND FAMILY: A SACRED BOND OF LOVE

Enter into wedlock, O people, that ye may bring forth one who will make mention of Me amid My servants. This is My bidding unto you; hold fast to it as an assistance to yourselves.

—*Bahá'u'lláh*, Bahá'í Prayers

There are many quotes in the Bahá'í writings on the subject of love, that essential human quality that makes life worth living. 'Abdu'l-Bahá spoke of it many times, often in talks he gave during his travels to different parts of the world. While in Europe, he proclaimed,

What a power is love! It is the most wonderful, the greatest of all living powers.

Love gives life to the lifeless. Love lights a flame in the heart that is cold. Love brings hope to the hopeless and gladdens the hearts of the sorrowful.

In the world of existence there is indeed no greater power than the power of love. When the heart of man is aglow with the flame of love, he is ready to sacrifice all—even his life. In the Gospel it is said God is love.[1]

'Abdu'l-Bahá, in this same passage, goes on to explain the station of true love among believers. He states,

The love which exists between the hearts of believers is prompted by the ideal of the unity of spirits. This love is attained through the knowledge of God, so that men see the Divine Love reflected in the heart. Each sees in the other the Beauty of God reflected in the soul, and finding this point of similarity, they are attracted to one another in love. This love will make all men the waves of one sea, this love will make them all the stars of one heaven and the fruits of one tree. This love will bring the realization of true accord, the foundation of real unity.[2]

In marriage, as in all human relationships, we need the kind of love that can build a *"foundation of real unity."* How do we attain this love? In the quote above, we learn that *"this love is attained through the knowledge of God."* It follows, then, that true love between people is intimately connected with the love of God. Through this love, *"each sees in the other the Beauty of God reflected in the soul."* Regarding what constitutes a true Bahá'í marriage, 'Abdu'l-Bahá writes, *"The true marriage of Bahá'ís is this, that husband and wife should be united both physically and spiritually, that they may ever improve the spiritual life of each other, and may enjoy everlasting unity throughout all the worlds of God. This is Bahá'í marriage."*[3]

What does it mean to *"improve the spiritual life of each other"?* Surely, in some ways, it must mean that we would support and encourage each other in our spiritual quest, that we would be patient with each other as we struggle to understand spiritual truths, and that we would consult with each other in order to make good decisions—decisions that conform not only to the principles of the Faith, but to the spirit of the Faith as well. Through our willingness to carry out these actions, we acquire the tools necessary to build the foundation of real unity spoken about by 'Abdu'l-Bahá and we expand our understanding of what love truly means.

When love is a part of marriage, the decision to have children is an expression of that love. In the Bahá'í writings the stations of marriage and family are joined together in a sacred bond. It is essential to our understanding as parents that we consider how Bahá'u'lláh, in the same sentence in which He speaks of marriage, also calls upon us to have children who will know and love God. *"Enter into wedlock, O people,"* He states, *"that ye may bring forth one who will make mention of Me amid My servants."* He follows with the injunction: *"This is My bidding unto you; hold fast to it as an assistance to yourselves."*[4]

Marriage, in another part of this passage, is described as *"a fortress for well-being."* In this fortress, children grow up safe and strong. When love for each other and love for God is the foundation of marriage and the raising of children, the benefits touch everyone in the family. Likewise, when children are trained to remember their Creator, they are more likely to be loving and considerate toward their parents. This would, indeed, be *"an assistance"* to us if we could but look into the future and see our lives unfold.

'Abdu'l-Bahá, in his many letters to Bahá'ís throughout the world, enabled them to expand their knowledge of Bahá'u'lláh's revelation and encouraged them to rise to greater heights of spiritual understanding. In his unique and loving communications, he often made the recipients feel like his very own children. To a newly married couple, he wrote,

> *O ye my two beloved children! The news of your union, as soon as it reached me, imparted infinite joy and gratitude. Praise be to God, those two faithful birds have sought shelter in one nest. I beseech God that He may enable them to raise an honored family, for the importance of marriage lieth in the bringing up of a richly blessed family, so that with entire gladness they may, even as candles, illuminate the world. For the enlightenment of the world dependeth upon the existence of man. If man did not exist in this world, it would have been like a tree without fruit. My hope is that you both may become even as one tree, and may, through the outpourings of the cloud of loving-kindness, acquire freshness and charm, and may blossom and yield fruit, so that your line may eternally endure.*
>
> *Upon ye be the Glory of the Most Glorious.*[5]

In this letter 'Abdu'l-Bahá educates us all as to the importance of marriage. He writes, *"the importance of marriage lieth in the bringing up of a richly blessed family."* We sometimes think that our own small family is of no real importance to the world or has little impact on the problems that it faces. 'Abdu'l-Bahá tells us that one richly blessed family can *"illuminate the world."* In the material sense we may not be able to discover the effect our family has on other people. In the spiritual sense, however, we can only believe what 'Abdu'l-Bahá tells us is true—that somehow the efforts we put forth to create a loving family are much more significant than we may have ever dreamed. Its example may even bring light to a darkened world, as 'Abdu'l-Bahá expresses it, *"Love is the light that guideth in darkness. . . ."*[6]

When we think of the people closest to us, we recognize that their *"light"* guides our way when we are most in need of love and assistance. They are *"even as candles"* that warm our hearts and minds. If, as individuals, we are able to assist each other in this way, how much more would a strong, caring couple touch the lives of those around them? How, too, would a loving family's presence impact the happiness and welfare of the entire community? We can never know what our one tiny flame can contribute to the world. One candle, by itself, is not aware of the light that it brings forth, but we know by observation that a single flame can illuminate an entire room. How much more brightly would it shine if joined with several other candles?

A beautiful vision of a spiritual family is given to us by 'Abdu'l-Bahá in this final quote on marriage. He writes,

As to thy question concerning the husband and wife, the tie between them and the children given to them by God. . . the tie between them is none other than the Word of God. Verily, it causeth the multitudes to assemble together and the remote ones to be united. Thus the husband and wife are brought into affinity, are united and harmonized, even as though they were one person. Through their mutual union, companionship and love great results are produced in the world, both material and spiritual. The spiritual result is the appearance of divine bounties. The material result is the children who are born in the cradle of the love of God, who are nurtured by the breast of the knowledge of God, who are brought up in the bosom of the gift of God, and who are fostered in the lap of the training of God. Such children are those of whom it was said by Christ, "Verily, they are the children of the Kingdom![7]

4

PREGNANCY: THE SOUL AND THE BEGINNING OF SPIRITUAL EDUCATION

O my Lord, I dedicate that which is in my womb unto Thee.
Then cause it to be a praiseworthy child in Thy Kingdom
and a fortunate one by Thy favor and Thy generosity;
to develop and to grow up under the charge of Thine education.
Verily, Thou art the Gracious! Verily, Thou art the Lord
of Great Favor!

—'*Abdu'l-Bahá*, Bahá'í Prayers

Pregnancy is a wonderful miracle. How fortunate are the children who are loved into being and whose presence is eagerly awaited by their parents! I remember how happy my husband and I were when we learned I was pregnant. We soon realized that God had entrusted to our care a tiny being who depended on our love for its physical and spiritual needs. We understood that there were many things we needed to learn in order to fulfill this sacred responsibility. But, most of all, we felt thankful for this blessing, a blessing we would cherish all our lives.

Within every child lies a wonderful mystery, the mystery of the human soul. Bahá'u'lláh describes it in these words: *"Know, verily, that the soul is a sign of God, a heavenly gem whose reality the most learned of men hath failed to grasp, and whose mystery no mind, however acute, can ever hope to unravel. It is the first among all created things to declare the excellence of its Creator, the first to recognize His glory, to cleave to His truth, and to bow down in adoration before Him. If it be faithful to God, it will reflect His light, and will, eventually, return unto Him."*[1] God bestows this knowledge upon His children to help us comprehend our true reality. We marvel at the meaning of the words. We also recognize from this passage that by giving us a child God has bestowed upon us a *"heavenly gem,"* a priceless treasure, and a *"sign of God."*

'Abdu'l-Bahá, in his own unique way, offers us another description of the soul. He states, *"Man—the true man—is soul, not body; though physically man belongs to the animal kingdom, yet his soul lifts him above the rest of creation. Behold how the light of the sun illuminates the world of matter: even so doth the Divine Light shed its rays in the kingdom of the soul. The soul it is which makes the human creature a celestial entity!"*[2] And, in another passage, he states, *"The soul is not a combination of elements, it is not composed of many atoms, it is of one indivisible substance and therefore eternal. It is entirely out of the order of the physical creation; it is immortal!"*[3] As parents, we have the distinct honor of nurturing this very special part of our children, this mysterious, wonderful, and eternal part that we call the *"soul."* This is the true meaning of spiritual education.

What, then, is our responsibility toward our unborn child, our *"heavenly gem,"* during these earliest days of its existence? Since the soul of the child is present at conception, it requires spiritual nourishment from the very beginning of life. This spiritual nourishment, as well as physical nourishment, begins with the mother. A letter written on behalf of the Universal House of Justice states, *"Her attitude, her prayers, even what she eats and her physical condition have a great influence on the child when it is still in the womb."*[4] As she becomes more aware of this influence, both physical and spiritual, she can better meet the needs of her child.

One of the most important ways that a mother can provide her child with spiritual nourishment is to pray for it. By reciting the Bahá'í prayer for expectant mothers, the mother learns to nurture her child spiritually. She learns to ask God to help her child become *"praiseworthy"* and *"fortunate."* She learns to rely upon God's *"favor"* and *"generosity."* And, finally, she learns that God is, indeed, the *"Lord of Great Favor."* As she learns these things, she embarks upon her role as mother.

The father, too, has an important role to play during this time. He should be supportive of his wife by loving and taking care of her. He should pray for her and for the baby. By reciting the prayers, the parents strengthen their love for God. By reciting the prayers, they grow in unity and learn to be thankful. By reciting the prayers, they nurture the soul of the child and connect its heart to God.

We can never truly appreciate the importance of these simple actions. We can only believe that there is a reason we must develop a relationship with God and express our love for Him in prayer. By praying for our child, our *"heavenly gem,"* we direct its soul toward its Creator. Love is an important part of this process. The parents' love for each other, their love for their unborn child, their love for God, and their awareness of His love for them are all necessary aspects of this process of growing spiritually. 'Abdu'l-Bahá emphasizes the importance of love in this process when he writes, *"Love is . . . the living link that uniteth God with man, that assureth the progress of every illumined soul."*[5] It is through this love that we come to know God.

As we feel our baby growing inside the womb, we stand in awe of the miracle of life, a miracle that has taken place time and again in the span of human existence. And we wonder—What will our baby be like? How will our lives change? How will we know what to do? We have numerous questions during these nine long months, but we are filled with the excitement and anticipation of what is yet to come. One thing we know for certain is that we must nurture our child both physically and spiritually. In the dictionary, we find that the term "nurture" means "to feed and protect, to support and encourage, and to educate." We know that we must do all of these things and that we must do them with love. We must also rely upon God to help us each step of the way.

It is through our knowledge and love of God that we begin to understand the spiritual part of ourselves and of our children, that part that cannot be seen. Bahá'u'lláh states, *"Verily I say, the human soul is, in its essence, one of the signs of God, a mystery among His mysteries."*[6] It is this part, this mystery of mysteries, that we seek to educate.

Bahá'u'lláh, in the Hidden Words, gives us a reassuring glimpse into the importance of spiritual growth. He states,

O Son of Man! I loved thy creation, hence I created thee. Wherefore, do thou love Me, that I may name thy name and fill thy soul with the spirit of life.[7]

5

INFANTS:
GOD'S PRECIOUS GIFT

*O Son of Bounty! Out of the wastes of nothingness, with the clay
of My command I made thee to appear, and have ordained
for thy training every atom in existence and the essence of all
created things. Thus, ere thou didst issue from thy mother's womb,
I destined for thee two founts of gleaming milk,
eyes to watch over thee, and hearts to love thee.*

—*Bahá'u'lláh*, Hidden Words

How can the birth of a baby be described? With awe and wonder, we gaze upon the face of our beloved child. We inhale the sweet fragrance from the small warm body. We touch the soft and delicate hands. Our eyes rest on the tiny rosebud lips, the dark and liquid eyes. We are a witness to the miracle of life and love in all its intensity swells up within us. With tears of joy, with thankfulness and humility, we accept this precious gift from God! For nine long months, we have waited, worried, hoped, and prayed for this tiny infant. And when, at last, the day arrives, we are so grateful, tired, and happy. *"Ere thou didst issue from thy mother's womb, I destined for thee two founts of gleaming milk, eyes to watch over thee, and hearts to love thee."* [1] How beautiful are the words of Bahá'u'lláh! And how well they express the love of parents for their children!

I remember what intense love I felt for my sons, even at that early hour. I vowed to do my best for them. I felt that I could even give my life if necessary. All of these feelings came rushing to my heart in one brief moment when their faces came in view. I know my husband felt the same way too. I felt a bond with all the other mothers in the world—mothers who bore their own children or who adopted them out of love or who lovingly raised them as foster parents—mothers who from time unrecorded had protected and loved their children and sacrificed for them.

And so we begin the exhausting but wonderful care of the new baby. What will the future hold for us? Will we be good parents? Will we be able to fulfill the dreams that we have for them? When my first son was born, I had been a Bahá'í for exactly one year. I tried to look into the future and imagine the kind of person I wanted him to be. I dreamed of raising a spiritual child, one who was loving, kind, and strong. I did not know how to accomplish that goal. The Bahá'í writings taught me what it meant to be a mother, but, more importantly, they taught me how to be a spiritual one. Bahá'u'lláh states, *"At the outset of every endeavour, it is incumbent to look to the end of it."* [2] The writings gave me a vision to see the end of it. I write this book to help other parents see the end of it through one mother's eyes. I raised my children with these beautiful writings. They gave me the hope and confidence that the goal God has given us of raising spiritual children is very real and very possible if only we could see it.

During the lifetime of 'Abdu'l-Bahá, many parents wrote to him with questions about raising children. Many of the writings that we have today about parenting are 'Abdu'l-Bahá's replies to those letters. Because of this, we have a wealth of information regarding every aspect of parenting. He emphasized the spiritual truths that are important at every age of a child's life, and he did it in a loving way that encourages and inspires. His life was filled with difficulties. His childhood was cut short because of the imprisonment of his father, Bahá'u'lláh, but his love for humanity never failed, and his love for children never faded. I thank God for these wonderful words that made such a difference in our family. I cannot imagine our lives without them.

The Duty of Parents

The writings of 'Abdu'l-Bahá have much to offer us in the way of hope and encouragement as we begin our new lives as parents. By reflecting upon the roles of mothers and fathers as described in the Bahá'í writings, we acquire the spiritual understanding that is necessary to begin this most important task.

One of the first responsibilities of parents is that of protection. 'Abdu'l-Bahá writes, *"Children must be most carefully watched over, protected and trained; in such consisteth true parenthood and parental mercy."*[3] To exhibit true parenthood, we must do our best to protect our children and to take care of their many needs. To exhibit true mercy, we must take care of their needs with an attitude of kindness and compassion.

One of the first ways that we take care of our children's needs is by providing them with the proper food, shelter, and clothing that are so necessary for their health and well-being. Newborn babies need special care. 'Abdu'l-Bahá writes, *"The child must, from the day of his birth, be provided with whatever is conducive to his health; and know ye this: so far as possible, the mother's milk is best for, more agreeable and better suited to, the child, unless she should fall ill or her milk should run entirely dry."*[4]

Proper nutrition is important for all ages. Parents should provide their children with food that is nutritious, natural, and well-balanced so that they will grow up to be healthy and strong. It is also interesting to note that science now confirms the advice that 'Abdu'l-Bahá gave us so many years ago regarding the benefit of mother's milk. Might it not be just a matter of time before science confirms that loving God is also good for children?

'Abdu'l-Bahá offers this additional counsel regarding the care we should give our children at the beginning of their lives. He writes,

Unless the child, in his earliest years, be carefully tended, whether in a material or a spiritual sense, whether as to his physical health or his education, it will prove extremely difficult to effect any changes later on. For example, if a child is not properly cared for at the beginning of life, so that he doth not develop a sound body and his constitution doth not flourish as it ought, his body will remain feeble, and whatever is done afterward will take little effect. This matter of protecting the health of the child is essential, for sound health leadeth to insights and sense perceptions, and then the child, as he learneth sciences, arts, skills, and the civilities of life, will duly develop his powers. . . .[5]

Another area of importance that parents should consider is the training of children. 'Abdu'l-Bahá writes, *"It is the duty of parents to perfectly and thoroughly train their children."*[6] In this passage, we observe that 'Abdu'l-Bahá chooses the word "*train*" instead of the word "teach." The meanings of these two words are quite different. The dictionary defines "teach" as "to impart knowledge," whereas "*train*" means "to develop or form the habits, thoughts, or behavior of a child by discipline and instruction." For parents to develop and form the habits, thoughts, and behavior of their children, they need considerable amounts of time, consistent effort, and loving patience. Furthermore, 'Abdu'l-Bahá tells us that we must train our children *"perfectly and thoroughly."* As we reflect upon these words, we can begin to understand the best ways to accomplish these goals.

The Mother's Role

The mother holds a very special place in the life of the child. "O thou servant of God!" writes 'Abdu'l-Bahá, *"Thou didst ask as to the education of children. Those children who, sheltered by the Blessed Tree, have set foot upon the world, those who are cradled in the Faith and are nurtured at the breast of grace—such must from the beginning receive spiritual training directly from their mothers."*[7]

In another passage, 'Abdu'l-Bahá writes, *"It is she who must, at the very beginning, suckle the newborn at the breast of God's Faith and God's Law, that divine love may enter into him even with his mother's milk, and be with him till his final breath."*[8] The mother's ability to profoundly influence the life of her child is quite evident. The physical nourishment and care that babies receive from their mothers at this young age affects their health far into the future. Likewise, the spiritual nourishment that babies receive from their mothers can prove so powerful as to last throughout their entire lives, even until their final breath. The mother's role is, therefore, unique because she is the very *first* educator of the child.

What particular human quality is necessary for a mother to nurture her children spiritually? *"Have for them an abundant love,"* counsels 'Abdu'l-Bahá, *"and exert thine utmost in training them, so that their being may grow through the milk of the love of God. . . ."*[9] How do we express abundant love? In many ways, abundant love is expressed through physical means. The importance of physical closeness between mother and baby during these formative years cannot be underestimated. Her gentle touch, her tender kisses, the intimacy of breastfeeding, and the smell of her milk all contribute to the baby's physical and emotional well-being. As she bathes and feeds her infant, changes countless diapers, and takes care of numerous needs, she expresses her deep love for her child. There is nothing more important in the child's life at this time than the love of the mother and the time they spend together. It is essential for the child's development.

From the very beginning of life, infants learn who they are and how they are accepted by the world through contact with their parents. What do babies learn about themselves when their mothers tenderly exclaim, "Your mommy loves you so much, sweetheart! You are so beautiful! Yes, you are, my darling! Do you know you are a precious child of God"? And what do children learn if her words are unloving or if they never hear words at all except for the hum of the TV set? Every word, every kiss, every moment is important to the helpless infant who is dependent on its parents for its every need. Even if they are fed, kept clean, and taken care of physically, babies must receive love in order to grow. It is the food of the soul.

One of the ways that a mother can express her love for her children is by teaching them the love of God. 'Abdu'l-Bahá writes, *"The mother must continually call God to mind and make mention of Him, and tell of His greatness . . . and rear the child gently, in the way of tenderness, and in extreme cleanliness. Thus from the very beginning of life every child will be refreshed by the gentle waftings of the love of God and will tremble with joy at the sweet scent of heavenly guidance. In this lieth the beginning of the process; it is the essential basis of all the rest."*[10]

How do we teach the love of God to infants and children? We can follow the advice of 'Abdu'l-Bahá when he writes, *"When the children are ready for bed, let the mother read or sing them the Odes of the Blessed Beauty, so that from their earliest years they will be educated by these verses of guidance."*[11] What are the *"Odes of the Blessed Beauty"*? The term *"Blessed Beauty"* is a title given to Bahá'u'lláh. An ode is a lyric poem that expresses exalted or enthusiastic emotion. And a lyric poem is defined as having the form of a song, especially one expressing the writer's feelings. To read or sing the heavenly words of Bahá'u'lláh with exalted and enthusiastic emotion, at any time of day, is a beautiful expression of love for God and imbues the child with heavenly *"verses of guidance."*

I remember those sweet times spent with my sons before they went to sleep at night. The times I sang to my sons or read them prayers were always very special times for us. They always looked forward to it. Even when they were much older, they would request a prayer, a Bahá'í song, or a beautiful Bahá'í quote set to music before they went to sleep at night or when they were sick and needed comfort. I always tried to tuck them in with kisses, prayers, and words of love.

I have always felt that being a woman was a special honor because it gave me the opportunity of becoming a mother. The writings helped me to understand how exceptional a role it really was. Shoghi Effendi writes, *"The task of bringing up a Bahá'í child, as emphasized time and again in Bahá'í writings, is the chief responsibility of the mother, whose unique privilege is indeed to create in her home such conditions as would be most conducive to both his material and spiritual welfare and advancement. The training which the child first receives through his mother constitutes the strongest foundation for his future development. . . ."*[12]

Should mothers, then, work outside the home or confine themselves to the raising of children? A letter from the Universal House of Justice addresses this important question. It states,

With regard to your question whether mothers should work outside the home, it is helpful to consider the matter from the perspective of the concept of a Bahá'í family. This concept is based on the principle that the man has primary responsibility for the financial support of the family, and the woman is the chief and primary educator of the children. This by no means implies that these functions are inflexibly fixed and cannot be changed and adjusted to suit particular family situations, nor does it mean that the place of the woman is confined to the home. Rather, while primary responsibility is assigned, it is anticipated that fathers would play a significant role in the education of the children and women could also be breadwinners. As you rightly indicated, 'Abdu'l-Bahá encouraged women to "participate fully and equally in the affairs of the world."[13]

Parents, through loving consultation, can decide what is best for their particular family circumstances.

Mothers, as we have learned, are extremely important in the spiritual education of their children. How does the role of mothers compare to all other forms of service that we are called upon to do for our Creator? 'Abdu'l-Bahá offers this impressive answer. He writes, *"O ye loving mothers, know ye that in God's sight, the best of all ways to worship Him is to educate the children and train them in all the perfections of humankind; and no nobler deed than this can be imagined."*[14] No nobler deed than this can be imagined!

What should our attitudes be, then, as mothers, for this bounty? Once again, 'Abdu'l-Bahá enlightens us. He writes,

O handmaids of the Merciful! Render ye thanks unto the Ancient Beauty that ye have been raised up and gathered together in this mightiest of centuries, this most illumined of ages. As befitting thanks for such a bounty, stand ye staunch and strong in the Covenant and, following the precepts of God and the holy Law, suckle your children from their infancy with the milk of a universal education, and rear them so that from their earliest days, within their inmost heart, their very nature, a way of life will be firmly established that will conform to the divine Teachings in all things.

For mothers are the first educators, the first mentors; and truly it is the mothers who determine the happiness, the future greatness, the courteous ways and learning and judgment, the understanding and the faith of their little ones.[15]

The Father's Role

We have learned much about the mother's role in the life of the child. What, then, is the father's role and how does it compare to the mother's? A letter written on behalf of the Universal House of Justice states, *"That the first teacher of the child is the mother should not be startling, for the primary orientation of the infant is to its mother. This provision of nature in no way minimizes the role of the father in the Bahá'í family. Again, equality of status does not mean identity of function."*[16]

Besides the important role he plays as described in the previous section, the father's role is also one of love. The father's love is extremely important to the tiny child. Its significance cannot be overemphasized. How do infants feel when their fathers hold them in their strong and gentle hands, smile at them tenderly, and speak to them in loving words? How special they must feel when their fathers love them and spend time with them! It just goes to show that both parents have important roles to play and to contribute to their child's development.

I have always felt that there was a reason God gave us two parents, even though many of us must face life with only one. The father's support of the mother in her physically demanding role, his assistance in taking care of the baby's many needs, his help with the finances and the maintenance of the house, and his presence in the child's life all contribute to the welfare of the family. Furthermore, a father teaches his children what it means to be a good man. If he has done a fine job, his sons will want to grow up to be like him and his daughters will want to marry someone with the same qualities. As the quote above states, *equality of status does not mean identity of function.* I know what my husband did for our sons. His was a unique role, different from mine, but equal. Because of his love and support, our family was happy and strong.

As children grow older, the father's role becomes more apparent. He will continue, at each stage of his children's lives, to guide and encourage them, and to teach and inspire them. It will require his time, his patience, and his dedication in order to raise good and loving children. But, most of all, it will require his love, the greatest gift that he can offer.

When it comes to raising children, single parents face a special challenge. Because they must take on the role of both mother and father, their parental responsibilities are twice as difficult and emotionally demanding. It is a role that seems almost impossible at times. This is where love can also play a part. When children feel truly loved and cared for by a parent, when they know that this parent is doing the best that he or she can, and when they are taught to love God and to appreciate life, they grow up with the understanding that they are fortunate to have such a parent, a parent who is hardworking, self-sacrificing, and strong. Sometimes all we can do in life, no matter what our circumstances, is the best that we can and then leave the rest up to God. With God, all things are possible.

Once again, we ask this question, "How do we show our children abundant love?" If we have learned how to love from our parents, we follow their example. Parents who are very affectionate toward their children, who hug them and kiss them, who hold them and spend time with them, teach their children, through their actions, that they are loved. We all know when we are truly loved by another person. 'Abdu'l-Bahá states, *"If I love you, I need not continually speak of my love—you will know without any words. On the other hand if I love you not, that also will you know—and you would not believe me, were I to tell you in a thousand words. . . . "*[17] Children need all the love that we can give them—both spoken and unspoken. If we did not have the benefit of loving parents, we can still learn to love and to take care of our children. We learn this through the knowledge of the love of God and through the examples of loving and caring individuals.

The way we train our children how to love is by loving them. They need to be taught the love of God, though, since they cannot see Him or hear Him. By praying with our children when they are small, we share with them the wonderful secret that they are heavenly beings created by a loving God. By protecting and training our children, and by tending to their material and spiritual needs, we teach them that they are human beings worthy of love and respect.

It will be the special times that we remember when our babies are grown—the fragrant smell of baby's breath, the happy, contented smiles when they are fed, the little yawns when they are sleepy, and those many moments both tender and sweet. May God bless our dear angels and watch over them so that they will grow to be loving and wise. And may love rise up from our hearts with joy when reciting this beautiful prayer,

O God! Rear this little babe in the bosom of Thy love, and give it milk from the breast of Thy Providence. Cultivate this fresh plant in the rose garden of Thy love and aid it to grow through the

showers of Thy bounty. Make it a child of the kingdom, and lead it to Thy heavenly realm. Thou art powerful and kind, and Thou art the Bestower, the Generous, the Lord of surpassing bounty.[18]

6

LITTLE CHILDREN: GEMS OF INESTIMABLE VALUE

O God, guide me, protect me, make of me a shining lamp and a brilliant star. Thou art the Mighty and the Powerful.

—*'Abdu'l-Bahá*, Bahá'í Prayers

How precious are little children! How beautiful and innocent, how sweet and loving! Their gentle laughter, their soft kisses, and their joy in little things enrapture us. It is an age filled with wonder and delight, one in which every moment should be cherished for so soon they are grown. We are thankful for these priceless gems, these rare and special gifts from God. We pray that God will help us to be spiritual parents and we look forward to the days ahead. It will be, we are certain, a wonderful journey.

As we go through life, we continue to learn what it means to be spiritual parents. The Bahá'í writings help us in this endeavor, as do memorable and spiritual experiences. Soon after I became a Bahá'í, I had the good fortune of attending a Bahá'í family life conference. It could not have come at a better time because my husband and I were thinking about starting a family and we did not know the Bahá'í teachings on parenting. Since we were both very new to the Faith, we were eager to learn more. I was hoping to gain a better understanding of Bahá'í parenting as well as deepen my knowledge of the Bahá'í writings.

As part of the conference program, a short tape recording was presented. It featured the voice of Hand of the Cause of God Abu'l-Qásim Faizi speaking on the education of children. In a very gentle and patient voice, he spoke the words that touched my heart. He said, "According to the writings of Bahá'u'lláh, a child given to any family in the whole world is a treasure-house of God. In this treasure-house there are jewels, precious jewels, entrusted by the Hand of God. Each child is different from another one. Therefore, the duty of parents and educators will be to explore this treasure-house, to find out the jewels, to polish them, and to make the whole world benefit by these jewels. . . . By jewels, I mean talents, capacities, potentialities given to the child."[1]

As I listened to these words, a new vision opened up before my eyes. Instead of viewing children as empty vessels, I began to picture them as beautiful gems full of promise. I realized that when a gemstone is pulled from the earth it looks only like a rough stone. But when the lapidary (gem cutter) carefully studies it, then cuts and polishes it, the inner beauty and brilliance of the stone are revealed, and it becomes a glittering jewel. As I listened to these words, I envisioned my own little baby like a gemstone in the palm of my hand, full of all the potentialities that God had given it, and I knew that my duty would be to gently and lovingly polish it until it revealed its splendors.

I believe that during this talk, Mr. Faizi was referring to the beautiful quote by Bahá'u'lláh when He states, *"The Great Being saith: Regard man as a mine rich in gems of inestimable value. Education can, alone, cause it to reveal its treasures, and enable mankind to benefit therefrom."*[2] When we read the Word of God, our souls, our minds, and our hearts are educated to look at life in a different way. This is what happened to me that day. Those symbolic words gave me the understanding of an inner truth, one that cannot be explained in any other way. They helped me to see this creation of God, the human being, in an entirely new light. They helped me to see myself in an entirely new light too. I wondered—"How many gifts are yet to be mined in me? How many in all of us"? It was a very short talk, but it influenced my ideas about parenting for years to come.

The writings offer us the means by which we can educate our children spiritually. What we endeavor to give our children is not just a mere set of words, but, rather, a new way of living, of thinking, and of being. When we teach our children how to love, how to pray, and how to treat others, we are helping them to acquire eternal spiritual attributes. We are like the lapidary carefully polishing our precious gems. How fortunate are we that God has entrusted to us so great a treasure!

Prayer

One of the first ways that we can polish our precious gems is to teach them how to pray. To understand prayer, we must first study the words of Bahá'u'lláh when He states,

Intone, O My servant, the verses of God that have been received by thee, as intoned by them who have drawn nigh unto Him, that the sweetness of thy melody may kindle thine own soul, and attract the hearts of all men. Whoso reciteth, in the privacy of his chamber, the verses revealed by God, the scattering angels of the Almighty shall scatter abroad the fragrance of the words uttered by his mouth, and shall cause the heart of every righteous man to throb. Though he may, at first, remain unaware of its effect, yet the virtue of the grace vouchsafed unto him must needs sooner or later exercise its influence upon his soul. Thus have the mysteries of the Revelation of God been decreed by virtue of the Will of Him Who is the Source of power and wisdom.[3]

Children understand that prayer is talking with God. I have found that children love to pray. It seems to make them very happy. In a loving letter to two believers, 'Abdu'l-Bahá wrote, *"Praised be God, ye two have demonstrated the truth of your words by your deeds, and have won the confirmations of the Lord God. Every day at first light, ye gather the Bahá'í children together and teach them the communes and prayers. This is a most praiseworthy act, and bringeth joy to the children's hearts: that they should, at every morn, turn their faces toward the Kingdom and make mention of the Lord and praise His Name, and in the sweetest of voices, chant and recite."*[4]

In this same letter, 'Abdu'l-Bahá goes on to explain the meaning of prayer. He states, *"These children are even as young plants, and teaching them the prayers is as letting the rain pour down upon them, that they may wax tender and fresh, and the soft breezes of the love of God may blow over them, making them to tremble with joy."*[5] 'Abdu'l-Bahá assists us in the understanding and appreciation of many spiritual concepts through his use of nature as a symbol for the spiritual world. And what a beautiful depiction of prayer he offers! Who among us has had the opportunity of dancing in a soft summer shower, of watching a thousand sparkling raindrops fall gently from the sky, and of smelling the air as it turns fresh and clean? Who remembers a sense of peace and beauty there, like the world was new again and we were part of it? Did we not *"tremble with joy"*? Is it possible that prayer can be like that, especially for the pure of heart?

When we gaze upon the sweet faces of little children reciting their first prayers, we learn, from their illumined countenance, that their souls understand the words, even if their minds, as yet, do not. Bahá'u'lláh explains this mysterious truth when He states, *"The understanding of His words and the comprehension of the utterances of the Birds of Heaven are in no wise dependent upon human learning. They depend solely upon purity of heart, chastity of soul, and freedom of spirit."*[6] The prayers *"bringeth joy to the children's hearts."* They give children a vision of their own true selves, they provide them with the knowledge of the spiritual qualities they have yet to attain, and they offer their thirsty souls a drink from the soul-reviving showers of the love of God.

Children enjoy saying prayers, especially when they have learned them by heart. When they are young, it is easier to learn prayers a little at a time. Shoghi Effendi writes, *"There is no objection to children who are as yet unable to memorise a whole prayer learning certain sentences only."*[7] When parents take the time to teach their children how to pray, they foster a spiritual bond between parent and child. Helping our children learn to pray is a sincere expression of love.

What prayers should we teach our children? Shoghi Effendi writes, *"Choose excerpts from the Sacred Words to be used by the child rather than just something made up. Of course prayer can be purely spontaneous, but many of the sentences and thoughts combined in Bahá'í writings of a devotional nature are easy to grasp, and the revealed Word is endowed with a power of its own."*[8]

There is a great difference between Bahá'í prayers and the prayers I learned growing up. I experienced an example of this one day with my own children. My son was only five years old when a young friend of ours, who was eight at the time, came to stay at our house overnight. Before the children went to sleep that evening, they took the time to say their prayers. *"O God, guide me, protect me,"* my son recited, putting great emphasis on each word as he spoke, *"make of me a shining lamp and a brilliant star. Thou art the Mighty and the Powerful."*[9]

I observed that when he finished, the eyes of his little friend widened and he looked at my son in amazement. I do not know what he was thinking, but the beauty of that simple prayer seemed to touch his pure young heart. I think he and my son felt a power in those sweet words that night. Whenever I hear this prayer, it always reminds me of my sons when they were little. It is special to me, because it is the very first prayer my sons ever learned.

Singing the prayers is also a wonderful way to learn them. 'Abdu'l-Bahá writes, *"The art of music is divine and effective. It is the food of the soul and spirit. Through the power and charm of music the spirit of man is uplifted. It has wonderful sway and effect in the hearts of children, for their hearts are pure and melodies have great influence in*

50

them."[10] If music can uplift the spirit, would prayers set to music have even more influence? I recall the face of a little four-year-old girl who was new to her Bahá'í class. She had not been raised a Bahá'í and was very shy at first, hiding behind her mother's legs. After her class learned Bahá'í songs and prayers, however, she became more comfortable and was soon seen singing these prayers with a joyful and heavenly expression on her face.

'Abdu'l-Bahá encourages us to set the Bahá'í writings to music. He states, *"Play and sing out the holy words of God with wondrous tones in the gatherings of the friends, that the listener may be freed from chains of care and sorrow, and his soul may leap for joy and humble itself in prayer to the realm of Glory."*[11] A letter from the Universal House of Justice also states,

> *It is entirely proper to set prayers to music, and the friends are free to sing prayers in unison. Indeed, assuming that the music is appropriate and that the believers do not make a ritual out of it.*
>
> . . .
>
> *We would assume also that the friends will always keep in mind that whether read, chanted or sung, prayer should be uttered with a proper sense of reverence.*[12]

The opportunity to teach our children how to pray is a wonderful blessing. So is praying for them. We should remember to say prayers for our children each day. These prayers not only nurture our children's souls, but also encourage us to see them as spiritual beings. They serve as spiritual patterns to help guide us in our parenting.

Reverence

Reverence is an important aspect of faith. It is defined in the dictionary as "a feeling of deep respect tinged with awe." Reverence is an attitude of deep devotion and sincere love for our Creator, a state of intense listening for the voice of God. As for myself, I do not think I understood the concept of reverence in its deepest sense until I had the honor of going on pilgrimage. Bahá'í pilgrimage takes place in Haifa and 'Akká, Israel, where the Bahá'í shrines and the administrative center of the Faith are located. Bahá'ís go on pilgrimage to experience the beauty, the history, and the sacredness of this place. Pilgrimage, for our family, was a unique and spiritual experience. Having the opportunity to visit the Bahá'í shrines was a great bounty and something never to be forgotten. I would like to share some of that experience with you now.

When we arrived at the Bahá'í properties, our eyes were immediately drawn to the intricately crafted gates that opened before us. As we entered the gardens, we experienced a different world, one of great peace and beauty. The many plants and flowers that lined the garden paths delighted our eyes with beautiful patterns and colors. As we walked down the crushed tile paths, we slowed our steps and felt encouraged to leave the world behind. We took notice of the bright blue sky, of the birds singing in the trees, and of the wind blowing through the softly swaying branches. We experienced heightened feelings of excitement, of intense longing, and of a profound sense of awe as each step brought us closer to the beautiful shrine before us.

Our guide explained what we should do. She very lovingly told us that we should remove our shoes before we entered the shrine, that we should pray silently so as not to disturb others, and that we should back out of the door of the shrine when we left as a sign of respect. Other than that, we could pray however we wished—sitting, standing, kneeling, or prostrated with our foreheads touching the floor. We slowly removed our shoes, felt the cool marble tiles beneath our feet, and walked quietly toward the entrance.

As we entered the shrine, we were immediately struck by the sweet scent of roses that lingered in the air. Inside, everything was simple and clean. Soft Persian carpets in gemlike colors warmed the floors. Smooth white walls glowed with a heavenly light. We carefully sat down facing the inner shrine. We began to pray. It was so peaceful there. We soon came to realize that just being in this holy place felt like prayer itself! 'Abdu'l-Bahá writes, *"You have asked about visiting holy places and the observance of marked reverence toward these resplendent spots. Holy places are undoubtedly centres of the outpouring of Divine grace, because on entering the illumined sites associated with martyrs and holy souls, and by observing reverence, both physical and spiritual, one's heart is moved with great tenderness. . . ."*[13]

Every person has an individual experience in the shrines. I am also certain that many people share a sense of peace there, of being loved by God, and of the deepest awareness of reverence that they have ever known. I have been there when Bahá'í parents brought their little children to the Shrine of the Báb. These little ones exhibited such a sweet sense of reverence that it brought tears to my eyes. Holding their parents' hands, they walked up slowly to the sacred threshold, the opening of the inner chamber where the remains of the Báb lie enshrined. They knelt down slowly before it, kissed the ledge on which vases of fresh flowers sat, and touched their little foreheads to the top of it as a sign of respect. Then they got up, walked backward very carefully, and sat down with their parents to say their prayers. It seemed like the most natural thing in the world for them to be reverent and to say prayers. But I knew that they had been trained perfectly and thoroughly regarding their behavior in the shrines by their parents. The very littlest ones were brought in only for a short time so that their parents could sit with them and teach them how to pray.

Children often learn by example. I was touched by a story about the young children of an important Israeli official who came to visit the Bahá'í gardens and the Shrine of the Báb. The children were very excited to be in such beautiful gardens. When it came time to enter the shrine, however, their parents told them to be very quiet and respectful once inside. After they had stayed a few minutes inside the shrine, the children noticed that their Bahá'í guides were bending over slightly and, very carefully, backing out of the shrine as they left. The children, without being told, followed their example and, very quietly and respectfully, bowed down and backed out of the shrine. They were so young and did not understand the significance of the place they were visiting, but I like to think that these pure little souls will be blessed for eternity by showing such reverence in the Shrine of the Báb.

Although we do not have the shrines near us in order to feel reverent, we must still try to acquire that same quality of devotion and respect when we read our prayers and find a way to teach it to our children. It is a matter of making that time special and sacred. It is leaving the world behind for a few moments so that we can focus on our spiritual needs. It is taking the time to teach our children that

God loves them, that it is important to pray, and that they are worthy of this special time for communing with God. Is there anything more wonderful in the whole world than the sound of little children saying their first prayers? To me, it is like the sound of angels singing.

Children's Behavior at Bahá'í Gatherings

There are many ways to teach our children how to practice reverence. Bahá'í gatherings, particularly Feasts and Holy Days, give us opportunities to do this. Bahá'í Feasts are community gatherings for Bahá'ís that take place every nineteen days and there are nine Holy Days in the Bahá'í year. When children go to Feast or Holy Days where Bahá'í prayers and writings are being read, they should be trained to sit quietly and reverently. Of course, much depends upon their age and level of maturity. Parents should explain that this is a special time when the community comes together to worship God and, during the Feast, to talk about community affairs. Those who organize the Feast should try to take young children into account when they plan the length of the readings. Feast hosts should also try to start the meeting on time since young children tire quickly and older children have to get up early for school the next day.

There are many ways that we can try to practice reverence and courtesy. For example, we could wait to walk into a room while prayers are being said, we could greet everyone with a friendly face, we could try to be on time so that we do not interrupt the readings, and we could show reverence for the holy writings by never placing them directly on the floor. I sometimes envision the holy words as if they are bound in pages of gold inlayed with precious gems. It helps me to realize their true significance and to treat them accordingly.

Children should be taught that the Bahá'í writings are to be revered and that there are times when they should conduct themselves in a reverent manner. It is for every individual to reflect upon the writings and to try to determine how they can best observe reverence and courtesy, and set an example for their children, as 'Abdu'l-Bahá explains, *"by observing reverence, both physical and spiritual, one's heart is moved with great tenderness. . . ."*

A letter written on behalf of the Universal House of Justice offers guidance regarding children's behavior at Bahá'í gatherings. It states,

> *The House of Justice has instructed us to say that children should be trained to understand the spiritual significance of the gatherings of the followers of the Blessed Beauty, and to appreciate the honour and bounty of being able to take part in them, whatever their outward form may be. It is realized that some Bahá'í observances are lengthy and it is difficult for very small children to remain quiet for so long. In such cases one or other of the parents may have to miss part of the meeting in order to care for the child. The Spiritual Assembly can also perhaps help the parents by providing for a children's observance, suited to their capacities, in a separate room during part of the community's observance. Attendance at the whole of the adult celebration thus becomes a sign of growing maturity and a distinction to be earned by good behavior.*
>
> *In any case, the House of Justice points out that parents are responsible for their children and should make them behave when they attend Bahá'í meetings. If children persist in creating a disturbance they should be taken out of the meeting. This is not merely necessary to ensure the properly dignified conduct of Bahá'í meetings but is*

an aspect of the training of children in courtesy, consideration for others, reverence, and obedience to their parents.[14]

Young parents should be diligent in teaching their children about courtesy, consideration for others, reverence, and obedience. Two mothers I know are innovative as well. They teach their young children the proper behavior at Feasts by playing the "Feast game." It is a game of pretend. The mothers and children pretend that they are going to go to Feast. First they pretend that they are taking a bath and putting on their best clothes. Then they pretend that they are getting in the car and taking a Bahá'í friend along. They practice getting there early so that the meeting can start on time. They practice saying "Alláh-u-Abhá" to greet all of their friends, a phrase that means "God is Most Glorious" in Arabic. And then they practice sitting respectfully during prayers and walking up to the front of the room to say their prayers out loud during the devotional portion of the Feast. They practice sitting and listening to the Feast letter during the administrative portion, after which they pretend to go to their class. They talk about what is proper behavior in someone's home. And, finally, they pretend that they are eating delicious refreshments during the social portion.

My friends have found that their children enjoy this game very much and, because of it, they look forward to attending Feast. Our own young son, when he was five years old, would happily get all cleaned up for Feast, comb his hair, put on his best clothes, and then, five minutes into the spiritual portion, fall soundly asleep for the remainder of the Feast. The very next Feast he would do the same thing all over again. It is only years later that I realize how much he must have loved those prayers and holy writings. They are a comfort to him even now.

Courtesy—Manners, Politeness, and Love

Courtesy occupies a very high station in the Bahá'í writings. Bahá'u'lláh states, *"O people of God! I admonish you to observe courtesy, for above all else it is the prince of virtues. Well is it with him who is illumined with the light of courtesy and is attired with the vesture of uprightness. Whoso is endued with courtesy hath indeed attained a sublime station. It is hoped that this Wronged One and everyone else may be enabled to acquire it, hold fast unto it, observe it, and fix our gaze upon it. This is a binding command which hath streamed forth from the Pen of the Most Great Name."*[15] And in another tablet He states, *"We, verily, have chosen courtesy, and made it the true mark of such as are nigh unto Him. Courtesy is, in truth, a raiment which fitteth all men, whether young or old. Well is it with him that adorneth his temple therewith, and woe unto him who is deprived of this great bounty."*[16]

Courtesy is a spiritual attribute that should adorn our souls. Courtesy is not just a nicety, a way of speaking or of acting in order to impress people. It is, in its spiritual context, a true consideration for others, a sincere helpfulness, a loving thoughtfulness, and a learned sensitivity that takes into account other people's feelings and needs. Courtesy, as defined by Bahá'u'lláh, is also a way to draw us nearer to God, as we learn from the quote: *"We, verily, have chosen courtesy, and made it the true mark of such as are nigh unto Him."*

Children who have been taught to be courteous are very pleasant, kind, friendly, and considerate. Because of these qualities, they are attractive to others. What should we teach our children about courtesy? Hand of the Cause of God Abu'l-Qásim Faizi, while speaking on the education of children, shared this advice. He said, "[Abdu'l-Bahá] says . . . 'Teach them manners, politeness, and love.'" He repeated, "Manners, politeness, and love." And then he added, "At present, we don't have the universal manners of the Bahá'í Faith, but whatever manners are prevailing in their own society, in their own community, and whatever manners which will be as near to the principles of the Bahá'í Faith as possible must be taught to the children, and politeness, and, above all, love."[17]

What are some of the manners that we should teach our children? I will share some of the things I think are important. First of all, we should train our children to say words like "please" and "thank you" as well as "excuse me." They should be trained to greet people politely, to speak when spoken to, to eat properly at the table (good table manners), to be helpful and friendly, to refrain from interrupting adults when they are talking, and to behave in whatever ways are considered polite and mannerly, depending on their culture. My hope for our sons was that they would learn how to exhibit true courtesy in whatever situation they found themselves, whether with family or friends, rich or poor, kings or queens, and in whatever country they lived in or visited. I wanted them to be able to be comfortable and loving with everyone, to always take into account the fact that they were raised Bahá'ís, and to try to act accordingly. My example for this vision was the person of 'Abdu'l-Bahá, the Exemplar of our Faith.

'Abdu'l-Bahá as our Example

In 1912, 'Abdu'l-Bahá came to visit the United States and Canada. He was sixty-eight years old. Howard Colby Ives, in his book *Portals to Freedom*, describes 'Abdu'l-Bahá's visit to Dublin, New Hampshire, and gives us a glimpse into his interactions with the people there.

Dublin is a beautiful mountain Summer resort where gathers each year a colony of wealthy intellectuals from Washington, D.C. and from various large centers. 'Abdu'l-Bahá's stay in that place for a period of three weeks offers another evidence of His unique power of adaptation to every environment; His dominant humility in every group, which, while seeming to follow He really led, and His manifest all-embracing knowledge.

Picture, if you can, this Oriental, fresh from more than fifty years of exile and prison life, suddenly placed in an environment representing the proudest culture of the Western world. Nothing in His life, one would reasonably presume, had offered a preparation for such a contact.

Not to His youth had been given years of academic and scholastic training. Not to His young manhood had been supplied those subtle associations during His formative years. Not upon His advancing age had been bestowed the comforts and leisure which invite the mind's expanse.

Quite the contrary, as I have endeavored to portray, His life had been a constant submission to every form of hardship and deprivation, when considered from a material standpoint alone. . . . The Bible and the Koran His only books.

How, then, can it be explained that in this environment He not only mingled with these highest products of wealth and culture with no slightest embarrassment to them or to Him, but He literally outshone them in their chosen field.

No matter what subject was brought up He was perfectly at home in its discussion, yet always with an undercurrent of modesty and loving consideration for the opinions of others. I have before spoken of His unfailing courtesy. It was really more than what that term usually connotes to the Western mind. The same Persian word is used for both reverence and courtesy. He "saw the Face of His Heavenly Father in every face" and reverenced the soul behind it. How could one be discourteous if such an attitude was held towards everyone!

The husband of 'Abdu'l-Bahá's hostess in Dublin, who, while never becoming an avowed believer, had many opportunities of meeting and talking with the Master, when asked to sum up his impressions of Him, responded, after a little consideration: "I think He is the most perfect gentleman I have ever known."

. . . It may be true, as He has many times reiterated, that the only true Life is that of the spirit, and that when one lives and moves and thinks constantly upon the spiritual plane, all things, both great and small, are done with perfectness.

Certainly, in my many contacts with this Master of Life, I never knew Him to fail in manifesting the highest qualities of conduct, whether in the realm of material action or in intellectual or spiritual teaching.[18]

The Importance of Virtues

We are fortunate to find the perfect example of virtues in the person of 'Abdu'l-Bahá. Although his life was filled with difficulties, he continued to shine forth spiritual qualities that were a source of joy and comfort to many people. Shoghi Effendi, in his book *God Passes*

By, describes 'Abdu'l-Bahá as *"incomparable in the spontaneity, the genuineness and warmth of His sympathy and loving-kindness shown to friend and stranger alike, believer and unbeliever, rich and poor, high and low, whom He met, either intimately or casually, whether on board ship, or whilst pacing the streets, in parks or public squares, at receptions or banquets, in slums or mansions, in the gatherings of His followers or the assemblage of the learned, He, the incarnation of every Bahá'í virtue and the embodiment of every Bahá'í ideal. . . ."*[19] As we study the extraordinary life of 'Abdu'l-Bahá, we are inspired to follow his example.

Training our children to acquire virtues is extremely important. It was so important to 'Abdu'l-Bahá that when asked the purpose of life, he answered, *"To acquire virtues."*[20] He writes, *"Every child must be trained in the things of the spirit, so that he may embody all the virtues and become a source of glory to the Cause of God."*[21] He also explains, *"Know thou that every soul is fashioned after the nature of God, each being pure and holy at his birth. Afterwards, however, the individuals will vary according to what they acquire of virtues or vices in this world."*[22]

The acquisition of divine virtues is important if our goal is to live a spiritual life. It also serves as preparation for the next life. 'Abdu'l-Bahá states,

> *Therefore, in this world he must prepare himself for the life beyond. That which he needs in the world of the Kingdom must be obtained here. Just as he prepared himself in the world of the matrix by acquiring forces necessary in this sphere of existence, so, likewise, the indispensable forces of the divine existence must be potentially attained in this world.*

. . . That divine world is manifestly a world of lights; therefore, man has need of illumination here. That is a world of love; the love of God is essential. It is a world of perfections; virtues, or perfections, must be acquired. That world is vivified by the breaths of the Holy Spirit; in this world we must seek them. That is the Kingdom of everlasting life; it must be attained during this vanishing existence.[23]

When we train our children to acquire divine virtues, we offer them a gift that lasts throughout the reaches of time.

How do we teach our young children to acquire virtues? A wonderful mother I know has thought of an interesting way to do this. She posts a "virtues chart" on her wall listing the names of virtues such as courtesy, kindness, and so on. When she notices her young children exhibiting these virtues, she happily accompanies them to the chart to pick out the virtues that they have displayed. She shared with me the fact that her four-year-old daughter was thrilled to see how many virtues she had actually exhibited after helping her mother by making her bed and putting away her toys. Although her children could not yet read, they were happy to know that their special virtue was up on the wall for all to see. If we have the desire to train our children to acquire spiritual virtues, we will surely find a way to do this. We must be creative in our parenting.

Kindness

Kindness is one of the divine virtues. *"Blessed is he who mingleth with all men in a spirit of utmost kindliness and love,"*[24] states Bahá'u'lláh. Although kindness seems a simple thing, it, nevertheless, must be taught to children. It is a learned behavior. *"Be ye sincerely kind,"* writes 'Abdu'l-Bahá, *"not in appearance only."*[25] The writings teach us to be kind to everyone, those we know as well as those we have yet to meet. *"Put into practice the Teaching of Bahá'u'lláh,"* counsels 'Abdu'l-Bahá, *"that of kindness to all nations. Do not be content with showing friendship in words alone, let your heart burn with loving kindness for all who may cross your path."*[26]

There are many opportunities in which to train our children to be kind. One of the ways we can do this is by training them how to share with others. This is not an easy task for little children, especially since they are primarily focused on their own needs. Training them to be kind is necessary, however, in order to expand their world to include the needs of others. Children should be taught to be helpful and kind to their friends as well as to members of their own family. Kindness, like courtesy, is thinking about the other person first. Children look to their parents as examples for this behavior. They observe how their parents treat people and learn to behave in the same way. If we want our children to be kind, we must be kind. If we want them to be loving, we must also be loving. As we attempt to train our children in these important virtues, we must also attempt to acquire them for ourselves. As we learn, they learn. As they grow, we grow. We help each other.

Another aspect of kindness to consider is our behavior toward animals. 'Abdu'l-Bahá writes, *"Train your children from their earliest days to be infinitely tender and loving to animals. If an animal be sick, let the children try to heal it, if it be hungry, let them feed it, if thirsty, let them quench its thirst, if weary, let them see that it rests."*[27] Bahá'u'lláh also advises, *"He should show kindness to animals, how much more unto his fellowman. . . .*"[28] As we go through life, we soon find that opportunities abound in which we can show kindness.

Even though we are taught to be kind to all people, there are times when we cannot be kind. This is an important lesson that children must eventually learn. 'Abdu'l-Bahá writes,

> *O ye beloved of the Lord! The Kingdom of God is founded upon equity and justice, and also upon mercy, compassion, and kindness to every living soul. Strive ye then with all your heart to treat compassionately all humankind—except for those who have some selfish, private motive, or some disease of the soul. Kindness cannot be shown the tyrant, the deceiver, or the thief, because, far from awakening them to the error of their ways, it maketh them to continue in their perversity as before. No matter how much kindliness ye may expend upon the liar, he will but lie the more, for he believeth you to be deceived, while ye understand him but too well, and only remain silent out of your extreme compassion.*[29]

Cleanliness

Another important virtue that we should acquire and train our children to acquire is cleanliness. 'Abdu'l-Bahá writes, *"The mother must continually call God to mind and make mention of Him, and tell of His greatness . . . and rear the child gently, in the way of tenderness, and in extreme cleanliness."*[30] When we study this passage carefully, we observe that 'Abdu'l-Bahá uses the word *"extreme"* when referring to cleanliness. The degree to which we practice cleanliness is very important. Though seemingly a physical thing, cleanliness is, nevertheless, connected to the spiritual realm. 'Abdu'l-Bahá writes,

My meaning is this, that in every aspect of life, purity and holiness, cleanliness and refinement, exalt the human condition and further the development of man's inner reality. Even in the physical realm, cleanliness will conduce to spirituality, as the Holy Writings clearly state. And although bodily cleanliness is a physical thing, it hath, nevertheless, a powerful influence on the life of the spirit. It is even as a voice wondrously sweet, or a melody played. . . . The purport is that physical cleanliness doth also exert its effect upon the human soul.[31]

What should we teach our children about cleanliness? Children should be taught to take care of their bodies, to bathe themselves in pure water, to brush their teeth, to comb their hair, and to wear clean clothes. In the notes to the Kitáb-i-Aqdas, we read the following: "The believers are exhorted in the Kitáb-i-Aqdas to bathe regularly, to wear clean clothes and generally to be the essence of cleanliness and refinement."[32] Bahá'u'lláh sets a very high standard for us in terms of cleanliness. In addition, He takes into account those people who, for specific reasons, are unable to follow these laws. He states, *"Whoso falleth short of this standard with good reason shall incur no blame."*[33]

If our physical cleanliness is so important, should not our homes and furnishings be clean as well? Bahá'u'lláh states, *"Thus hath it been ordained by One Who is Omniscient and All-Perceiving. He, verily, is desirous of refinement, both for you yourselves and for all that ye possess. . . ."*[34] It is evident, then, that we should take care of our children, our homes, and our furnishings with loving care. We should remember that our children are living things that we choose to bring into our lives. Our home is also like a living thing. It is the intimate space that surrounds our family. The atmosphere that we create in our home affects our health, our peace of mind, and our ability to function more fully in other areas of life.

Cleanliness has nothing to do with great amounts of wealth. It is a virtue that pertains to all people. It has to do with orderliness and simplicity. I recall a story of a woman who lived in a tiny village in the jungle. Her house was only a small hut with a dirt floor, but every morning she could be seen carefully sweeping out her home so that it would be clean. The simplest house can be the most welcoming if it is clean. The whole family should learn to clean the house. Little children could be taught to do small chores and learn to help in other ways.

While volunteering at the Bahá'í World Center in Israel, I had the opportunity to observe the high standard of cleanliness with which the Bahá'í buildings and gardens were maintained. Because of their beauty and cleanliness, these properties were a joy to behold. I know that if the gardens were not cared for, if trash were allowed to accumulate on the paths, if weeds were allowed to grow in the flower beds, or if the buildings were allowed to become dirty and cluttered, the atmosphere of peace and order would fade and a visitor's experience there would not be as pleasant or as spiritual.

I think that the Bahá'í properties are beautiful and welcoming, in large part, because thousands of people from all over the world volunteer their time to serve the Faith they love so well. Perhaps they could serve as examples of how we could help each other attain this high standard. For instance, we could volunteer to help paint the house of an elderly person or assist a single mother with yard work. Even little children can pitch in to pull a weed or two. There are many ways in which we can follow the teachings that Bahá'u'lláh has so generously given us. He states, *"Be ye the very essence of cleanliness amongst mankind. This, truly, is what your Lord, the Incomparable, the All-Wise, desireth for you."*[35]

Thankfulness

Thankfulness is a wonderful virtue. People who are thankful tend to be positive, happy people. An attitude of thankfulness should be taught to children when they are very young. One of the first ways we can teach them to be thankful is to point out the wonderful world that God has given them—the sky, the clouds, the trees, and the flowers. How thankful we should be for all of these things! He has given us plants to eat, water to drink, and people to love—oh, so many things! How many gifts can one day bring to count the things we are thankful for?

If children are taught thankfulness at an early age, they will not take things or people for granted. They will learn that, even in difficult times, they will still have many reasons to be thankful. They should learn to be thankful for the body that God gave them, for the people in their lives who care for them, and for the opportunity of learning new things. They should be thankful for the guidance that God has given them, for the knowledge of their own true selves, and for the wonderful example we have in the person of 'Abdu'l-Bahá.

It is our own attitude of thankfulness that forms our children's concept of it. We must remind ourselves every day to be thankful, even as we remind our children. One of the most important gifts that we can be thankful for is the blessing of Bahá'u'lláh, the Manifestation of God for this day. As parents, it is this blessing that enables us to give our children the gift of a spiritual education.

'Abdu'l-Bahá encourages us to appreciate these blessings when he states,

Do you realize how much you should thank God for His blessings? If you should thank Him a thousand times with each breath, it would not be sufficient because God has created and trained you. He has protected you from every affliction and prepared every gift and bestowal. Consider what a kind Father He is. He bestows His gift before you ask. We were not in the world of existence, but as soon as we were born, we found everything prepared for our needs and comfort without question on our part. He has given us a kind father and compassionate mother, provided for us two springs of salubrious milk, pure atmosphere, refreshing water, gentle breezes and the sun shining above our heads. In brief, He has supplied all the necessities of life although we did not ask for any of these great gifts. With pure mercy and bounty He has prepared this great table. It is a mercy which precedes asking.[36]

Mothers have a special responsibility when it comes to thankfulness. 'Abdu'l-Bahá writes,

O handmaids of the Merciful! Render ye thanks unto the Ancient Beauty that ye have been raised up and gathered together in this mightiest of centuries, this most illumined of ages. As befitting thanks for such a bounty, stand ye staunch and strong in the Covenant and, following the precepts of God and the holy Law, suckle your children from their infancy with the milk of a universal education, and rear them so that from their earliest days, within their inmost heart, their very nature, a way of life will be firmly established that will conform to the divine Teachings in all things.[37]

Discipline and Obedience

How do we rear our children so that their lives will conform to the divine teachings in all things? One of the ways that we can do this is by helping them to understand the importance of discipline and obedience. How do we accomplish this? As in all things, we accomplish this with love.

An important letter from the Universal House of Justice presented topics related to the education of children, the responsibilities of parents, and the role of the community in the life of the child. In all of this wonderful guidance, one particular phrase stood out in my mind. It was only three words: *"Love demands discipline. . . ."*[38] Discipline starts at a very young age. We must love our children enough to discipline them.

What does discipline mean? Discipline, as defined in the dictionary, is "training to act in accordance with rules." Training our children to act in accordance with the laws of God takes patience, firmness, and resolve. We should love them enough to expect them to exhibit good qualities such as courtesy, kindness, and helpfulness that will lead them to a happy and productive life. In order for this to happen, we must first train them to listen to us, to respect us, and to obey us. This is our responsibility as parents.

All good discipline begins with love. Love should be our guiding light when attempting to discipline our children. When children know that they are loved, they are more likely to behave appropriately. Shoghi Effendi writes, *"Love and kindness have far greater influence than punishment upon the improvement of human character."*[39] We should never discount the power of love and kindness on individuals, especially young children whose hearts are pure.

Parents who discipline with love use the technique of positive reinforcement. Positive reinforcement means that we encourage positive behavior by praising our children when they listen and behave well. 'Abdu'l-Bahá writes, *"Whensoever a mother seeth that her child hath done well, let her praise and applaud him and cheer his heart. . . ."*[40] Praise works wonders, as many teachers know. The more we emphasize our children's good behavior, the more we encourage them to exhibit that same behavior in the future. By acknowledging their efforts in accomplishing difficult things, we teach our children that they are worthy of attention and praise.

Along with positive reinforcement, good discipline requires us to exhibit gentleness and patience. We should remember that the world and all its exigencies are very new to little children. They need some time to learn the things we take for granted. In order to help them obey us, we should phrase our commands to them simply, lovingly, and firmly, and remember to say "thank you" afterward, just as we would to others. Sometimes it is also helpful to give them advance notice of what we are going to expect, so that they have time to adjust to the idea. At other times, we must patiently explain things over and over until they are able to understand and move forward. There will be times, however, when we ask our children to obey us quickly and without hesitation, as in circumstances involving their welfare and safety. Our attitude toward them should be one of loving guidance—helping and instructing them, encouraging them to exhibit appropriate behavior, and gently reminding them when they have forgotten. These are all a part of spiritual training.

Most children want to please their parents, especially when they know that their efforts will be acknowledged and praised. At times, however, acknowledgement and praise are not enough to eliminate inappropriate behavior. What should be done then? 'Abdu'l-Bahá offers this advice to mothers. He writes, *"And if the slightest undesirable trait should manifest itself, let her counsel the child and punish him, and use means based on reason, even a slight verbal chastisement should this be necessary. It is not, however, permissible to strike a child, or vilify him, for the child's character will be totally perverted if he be subjected to blows or verbal abuse."*[41]

It is sometimes difficult for us, coming from different cultures, to understand what 'Abdu'l-Bahá may have meant when he warns us against using certain forms of punishment. Mr. Faizi's comments on this matter may prove helpful. In his talk on the education of children, he stated that 'Abdu'l-Bahá said that we should never "beat" our children. He then went on to say, "The people of the world think that the child being beaten is well-educated or well-disciplined, and 'Abdu'l-Bahá says, 'Never!' . . . If, in their infant-hood, during the years of childhood, they cannot revenge that beating, they will do it in the future when they become stronger. . . . This child to have been beaten in the family is always afraid . . . always afraid that perhaps somebody else will beat him. Why should we do this to our children?"[42]

Mr. Faizi continued. "The second point was this," he said, "'Abdu'l-Bahá says after beating is tongue-lashing. Tongue-lashing is worse than beating. We should never use these words for the child, so that the child will be abashed, will be put to shame, will be belittled in front of others and in front of the family itself, always will think that the mother doesn't like him, the father doesn't like him. I'm unwanted in this family. . . . It is very bad. It kills the spirit of the child." Later, he went on to clarify, "By beating or tongue-lashing, I mean this—that which humiliates the child, will belittle the child, will demonstrate a certain despise in our hearts against the child. We must never do that."[43]

A letter written on behalf of the Universal House of Justice also addresses this issue. It states, *"While the discipline of children is an acceptable part of their education and training, such actions are to be carried out 'gently and patiently' and with 'loving care,' far removed from the anger and violence with which children are beaten and abused in some parts of the world."*[44]

We gather, therefore, that cruel beatings or harsh words that hurt children, that humiliate them, and that make them think we despise them, should never be used as punishment by parents. As parents we should not even consider such things. What, then, is allowable when it comes to punishing our children? A letter written on behalf of the Universal House of Justice states,

As to your question about the use of physical punishment in child training, although there is a Tablet of the Master which considers beating as not permissible, this does not necessarily include every

form of corporal punishment. In order to have a full grasp of the Master's attitude towards punishment, one has to study all His Tablets in this respect. For the time being no hard and fast rule can be laid down, and parents must use their own wise discretion in these matters until the time is ripe for the principles of Bahá'í education of children to be more clearly elucidated and applied.[45]

Along this same line, a letter written on behalf of Shoghi Effendi to an individual believer states,

Discipline of some sort, whether physical, moral or intellectual, is indeed indispensable, and no training can be said to be complete and fruitful if it disregards this element. The child when born is far from being perfect. It is not only helpless, but actually is imperfect, and even is naturally inclined towards evil. He should be trained, his natural inclinations harmonized, adjusted and controlled, and if necessary suppressed or regulated, so as to insure his healthy physical and moral development. Bahá'í parents cannot simply adopt an attitude of nonresistance towards their children, particularly those who are unruly and violent by nature. It is not even sufficient that they should pray on their behalf. Rather they should endeavor to inculcate, gently and patiently, into their youthful minds such principles of moral conduct and initiate them into the principles and teachings of the Cause with such tactful and loving care as would enable them to become "true sons of God" and develop into loyal and intelligent citizens of His Kingdom. This is the high purpose which Bahá'u'lláh Himself has clearly defined as the chief goal of every education.[46]

The writings enlighten us as to the true meaning of discipline. They show us that there are many things to consider as we attempt to discipline our children. One of the things that they encourage us to attain is wisdom when dealing with children. To acquire wisdom, we must put forth a considerable amount of time and effort. Even as new parents, however, we should never waver in our resolve to discipline our children, particularly in light of the fact that the lack of good discipline affects our children spiritually. Bahá'u'lláh states, *"The parents must exert every effort to rear their offspring to be religious, for should the children not attain this greatest of adornments, they will not obey their parents, which in a certain sense means that they will not obey God. Indeed, such children will show no consideration to anyone, and will do exactly as they please."*[47]

Children who are left to themselves to do as they please, without the proper guidance and discipline, have a difficult time as adults. In my opinion, it is one of the worst things that parents can do to their children. Children need strong parents. They need parents who set boundaries, who give them guidance, who explain expectations of behavior carefully and simply, and who follow through with punishment, if necessary, in ways that are appropriate to the child's age level and maturity. Of course, with little children, we should always be extremely gentle and patient, especially during the active ages of two and three. A certain degree of firmness, however, is required at every age. Parents who are afraid to do anything at all leave their children in limbo trying to figure things out for themselves or to grow up thinking that they can do whatever they want, always putting their needs before the needs of others. Good discipline is important. It helps children to eventually acquire the quality of self-discipline that is so necessary for a successful life.

Looking back so many years now, I realize that, compared to many parents today, we were quite firm with our children. As they grew older, we expected them to behave in certain ways at certain times. We expected them to be quiet and reverent while at Feasts and Holy Days, we expected them to be respectful of their parents, grandparents, and other adults, and we expected them to be courteous and mannerly in social situations. We expected them to work hard in school, to get good grades, and to respect their teachers. We also wanted them to be happy and free when they played with their friends, to laugh and to joke, to run and to play, and to have a good time. We tried to explain to our children in clear and simple terms what was expected of them when it came to rules and responsibilities. We tried to be patient and understanding with their attempts to follow this guidance. We were not always able to do this perfectly, but we tried our very best. We raised our sons with firmness and high expectations balanced with a great deal of love and affection.

One final thought that bears reflection concerns the word "punishment." It is interesting to note how some words are defined differently in different cultures. In Persian, for example, the word commonly used for "punishment" is "tanbíh." The original Arabic meaning for this word, however, is "to awaken." To "awaken" the child is a beautiful way to view our efforts toward disciplining and training our children. Mr. Faizi, in his talk, lovingly shared these enlightening words on the subject. He said, "Awaken the child to the situation by all the pleasant ways and means possible for the family. . . . The child is in darkness, does not understand. . . . If there is something happening to it [that] the child is in darkness, what should we do? We must bring a light and show him this. Awaken the child, always awakening."[48] With good training and oceans of love, we endeavor to awaken our children to the beautiful light of Bahá'u'lláh's teachings.

Patience and Support

Discipline is one important aspect of parenting. Another is taking the time to really get to know and understand our children. It is not easy to be good parents, to know exactly what to do at exactly the right time. Here again, we should be patient with ourselves even as we are patient with our children. Acquiring patience is a lifelong learning process, one in which we are challenged over and over again.

What is the meaning of patience? Patience is defined as "the bearing of misfortune, annoyance, or pain without complaint, loss of temper, or anger." It may also be defined as "calm endurance, tolerance, fortitude, or self-control." In dealing with difficulties with our own children, we could try some techniques that parents have found helpful in the past. For example, we could take a step back from the situation. We could try to compose ourselves. We could breathe deeply. And we could try to remember how loving and patient 'Abdu'l-Bahá would have been with us.

Parenting is a case of becoming—becoming something no one taught us how to become. Fortunately, we gain experience with each new day as we try our best to be good parents. The writings of the Faith assist us in this goal. We may also look for additional sources to aid us in our parenting, such as books on child rearing. Some of the most helpful books I read when my children were young were those that identified the developmental stages that children pass through as they grow older. By studying these stages, we are better equipped to understand why our children act the way they do. We should also understand that what is considered normal is really quite a large number of behaviors. I learned from observing my own children and the children of friends that they were all very different from one another. Some babies sleep through the night. Some never do. Some children walk early. Some walk late. My own sons started climbing everything in sight at nine months. Their internal clocks told them it was time to go out and explore the world. Another friend of mine had a baby who hardly crawled at all. He just sat there and observed the world. Then one day he got up and started walking. I can tell you from experience that all of these children turned out just fine. It did not matter if they followed "the norm" or not. I share this because it is important to understand that our children have their own time-tables for things. We must learn to listen to them.

Another lesson I learned is that mothers, fathers, and children all have unique personalities. Some are quiet. Some are talkative. Some have lots of energy. Some have little. When we become parents, we suddenly find ourselves with a new little personality in our lives who may or may not be like us. If their personalities are very different from our own, we may have difficulty responding to them appropriately. In order to understand our children, we must first acknowledge that they are unique creations of God. Then we must learn to appreciate those personality traits that are different from our own, just as we must learn to appreciate the unique differences in all people. The gem cutter must study the stone carefully. He must see all the possibilities latent within it before he can cut and polish it. He cannot hurry the task. He must first appreciate the beauty inside the stone.

When we recognize the jewels that our children possess, those talents and capacities that are uniquely their own, we can better help them to fulfill their potential. We must also remember that some talents and capacities that are not apparent when children are young may eventually reveal themselves as they grow older. Sometimes the very behavior that mothers and fathers find so irritating in young children may be the very strengths that they will need in the future, in order to advance in careers or to cope with adversity. We must remember that children *do* grow up, that they *will* learn the things they need to learn, and that parenting is not supposed to be easy. If it were, then every parent would be a good one.

Because of the many demands of parenting, it is important for new parents to find people who can be supportive of them. When I became a new mother, I had the good fortune of having a Bahá'í friend whose baby was the same age as mine. She was also new to the Faith so we had much in common. Since we could not be together often because of distance, we talked on the phone as much as possible. We had many long conversations about the Faith and about parenting. It was good to be able to talk to someone who was also trying to raise her baby spiritually.

Friends are very important to new parents. So is family. An extended loving family is worth their weight in gold. Grandparents who support parents and who give their grandchildren unconditional love are a great blessing. Their worth is priceless. I know what our extended family meant to our sons growing up. Without their grandparents, aunts, uncles, and cousins, their lives would not have been as rich nor would they have felt as loved. Our Bahá'í friends are also important because they provide us with the encouragement that we need in order to grow spiritually.

As we listen to our children, we begin to learn what they need. We must give our children what they need, not merely what they want. And what they really need is to be loved and to love. And what they really want, even if they are unable to express it, is to be good people and to love God. The real joy in life, the real happiness, comes from our relationships with others and our relationship with God. If we have that, we can get through the tough times. We can weather the storms of life. We are very fortunate if we have people who love and support us. We are also fortunate if we rely upon the Bahá'í writings to help us on our way.

Shoghi Effendi as a Child

In the book *The Priceless Pearl* by Rúhíyyih Rabbani, we are delighted to discover several stories about Shoghi Effendi as a young child. Rúhíyyih Rabbani recounts many interesting details about his life, including his special relationship with his grandfather, 'Abdu'l-Bahá, or the "Master" as he was lovingly referred to by Bahá'ís. These stories are particularly fascinating because they offer some insight into the topics we have covered. They also help us to appreciate the boy Shoghi Effendi was as well as the man he became.

Shoghi Effendi was a small, sensitive, intensely active and mischievous child. . . .

. . . It may sound disrespectful to say the Guardian was a mischievous child, but he himself told me he was the acknowledged ringleader of all the other children. Bubbling with high spirits, enthusiasm and daring, full of laughter and wit, the small boy led the way in many pranks; whenever something was afoot, behind it would be found Shoghi Effendi! This boundless energy was often a source of anxiety as he would rush madly up and down the long flight of high steps to the upper story of the house, to the consternation of the pilgrims below, waiting to meet the Master. His exuberance was irrepressible and was in the child the same force that was to make the man such an untiring and unflinching commander-in-chief of the forces of Bahá'u'lláh, leading them to victory after victory. . . . We have a very reliable witness to this characteristic of the Guardian, 'Abdu'l-Bahá Himself, Who wrote on a used envelope a short sentence to please His little grandson: "Shoghi Effendi is a wise man—but he runs about very much!"

It must not be inferred, however, that Shoghi Effendi was mannerless. Children in the East—how much more the children of 'Abdu'l-Bahá—were taught courtesy and manners from the cradle. Bahá'u'lláh's family was descended from kings and the family tradition, entirely apart from His divine teachings which enjoin courtesy as obligatory, ensured that a noble conduct and politeness would distinguish Shoghi Effendi from his babyhood.

In those days of Shoghi Effendi's childhood it was the custom to rise about dawn and spend the first hour of the day in the Master's room, where prayers were said and the family all had breakfast with Him. The children sat on the floor, their legs folded under them, their arms folded across their breasts, in great respect; when asked they would chant for 'Abdu'l-Bahá;

there was no shouting or unseemly conduct. Breakfast consisted of tea, brewed on the bubbling Russian brass samovar and served in little crystal glasses, very hot and very sweet, pure wheat bread and goat's milk cheese. Dr. Zia Baghdadi, an intimate of the family, in his recollections of these days records that Shoghi Effendi was always the first to get up and be on time—after receiving one good chastisement from no other hand than that of his grandfather![49]

Another touching story from this book is introduced by Rúḥíyyih Rabbani. She writes,

> By the signs Shoghi Effendi showed from earliest childhood and by his unique nature, he twined himself ever more deeply into the roots of the Master's heart. We are fortunate, indeed, to possess, from one of the earliest western believers, Ella Goodall Cooper, her own account of a meeting she witnessed between 'Abdu'l-Bahá and Shoghi Effendi at the time of her pilgrimage in March 1899, in the house of Abdullah Pasha:

> > One day . . . I had joined the ladies of the Family in the room of the Greatest Holy Leaf for early morning tea, the beloved Master was sitting in His favourite corner of the divan where, through the window on His right, He could look over the ramparts and see the blue Mediterranean beyond. He was busy writing Tablets, and the quiet peace of the room was broken only by the bubble of the samovar,

where one of the young maidservants, sitting on the floor before it, was brewing the tea.

Presently the Master looked up from His writing with a smile, and requested Ziyyih Khanum to chant a prayer. As she finished, a small figure appeared in the open doorway, directly opposite 'Abdu'l-Bahá. Having dropped off his shoes he stepped into the room, with his eyes focused on the Master's face. 'Abdu'l-Bahá returned his gaze with such a look of loving welcome it seemed to beckon the small one to approach Him. Shoghi, that beautiful little boy, with his exquisite cameo face and his soulful appealing, dark eyes, walked slowly toward the divan, the Master drawing him as if by an invisible thread, until he stood quite close in front of Him. As he paused there a moment 'Abdu'l-Bahá did not offer to embrace him but sat perfectly still, only nodding his head two or three times, slowly and impressively, as if to say—"You see? This tie connecting us is not just that of a physical grandfather but something far deeper and more significant." While we breathlessly watched to see what he would do, the little boy reached down and picking up the hem of 'Abdu'l-Bahá's robe he touched it reverently to his forehead, and kissed it, then gently replaced it, while never taking his eyes from the adored Master's face. The next moment he turned away, and scampered off to play, like any normal child. . . . At that time he was 'Abdu'l-Bahá's only grandchild . . . and, naturally, he was of immense interest to the pilgrims.[50]

This precious child, so full of energy, so full of life, and so full of spirit would eventually become the man who would design the beautiful gardens around the Bahá'í shrines, who would work tirelessly for the development of the Faith throughout the world, and who would touch our lives with his guidance and vision. The many stories recounted about the Guardian and his beloved grandfather, 'Abdu'l-Bahá, prove extremely valuable for us to study. Many of them offer us a glimpse into the life of the family of 'Abdu'l-Bahá and show us how they persevered in spite of intense trials. These stories offer us hope that we can also persevere in spite of intense difficulties in order to make the world a better place by raising spiritual children.

The Value of Love and Affection

There is nothing more valuable in children's lives than the love and affection they receive from their parents. Love and affection are crucial to children's mental, emotional, and spiritual development. The most wonderful benefit of being a parent is having the opportunity to shower our children with love and affection and to receive them in return. It is this loving relationship that enables us to appreciate the true meaning of life and to be thankful for the experience of parenting. It is this relationship that helps us to realize that we are profoundly blessed, as parents, and that life is, indeed, a miracle.

The way we show our children love and affection is by spending time with them. Our sons learned that their father loved them when he played with them. They liked to sit on his lap or wrestle with him or run around the yard catching a ball. They were happy just to be near him. He showed them affection in other ways, also, by kissing them and holding them, and by rocking them to sleep. By enjoying our children, by laughing and having fun with them, by cuddling them when we read them stories, and by watching them as they play with friends, we build the bonds of love that are the foundation of our relationship for years to come.

Love is the most powerful force in a child's life. Our love for our children helps them to understand the concept of a loving God. Our love for our children teaches them the importance of loving others. By giving our children love and affection, we help them to become the loving and caring adults we dream they will become. Loving and training our children are the most important contributions we can make to the world and teaching them to love God is the most important gift that we can give them.

'Abdu'l-Bahá helps us to appreciate the importance of educating and training children when he writes,

> Among the greatest of all services that can possibly be rendered by man to Almighty God is the education and training of children, young plants of the Abhá Paradise, so that these children, fostered by grace in the way of salvation, growing like pearls of divine bounty in the shell of education, will one day bejewel the crown of abiding glory.
>
> It is, however, very difficult to undertake this service, even harder to succeed in it. I hope that thou will acquit thyself well in this most important of tasks, and successfully carry the day, and become an ensign of God's abounding grace; that these children, reared one and all in the holy Teachings, will develop natures like unto the sweet airs that blow across the gardens of the All-Glorious, and will waft their fragrance around the world.[51]

85

Reflecting upon the days when our children were young, I can truthfully say that our sons were the greatest joy of our lives and spending time with them was our greatest happiness. We loved our children so very much and often told them that we did. They made us feel loved too. Because of them, we learned to be more loving. Because of them, we tried harder to be good Bahá'ís.

And now, although we love, respect, and enjoy the adults they have become, sometimes, just sometimes, we wish for just one day to have them small again, to hug them and kiss them, to hold them on our laps and hear their sweet baby voices say, "I love you, Mommy" and "I love you, Daddy." These are among the sweetest words in all the world. Dear friends, enjoy your children, your treasured gems from God, and train them in the ways of love, for children are only little for a little while, and the time with them is precious.

7

SCHOOL-AGE CHILDREN: ROSES OF ONE GARDEN

O God! Educate these children. These children are the plants
of Thine orchard, the flowers of Thy meadow, the roses of Thy garden.
Let Thy rain fall upon them; let the Sun of Reality shine upon them
with Thy love. Let Thy breeze refresh them in order that they may be
trained, grow and develop, and appear in the utmost beauty.
Thou art the Giver. Thou art the Compassionate.

—*'Abdu'l-Bahá*, Bahá'í Prayers

So quickly the time has arrived when our children are old enough to start school! How small they seem clutching their lunch bags, admiring their new pencils, their eyes aglow with the excitement of a brand new day! And how many are the emotions that stir within us when we watch them as they leave for school! Tenderly, we smile at them and wave goodbye, taking note of their small shining faces, their little hands upraised in greeting, and their wide eyes eager to embrace the world.

We are ready now, as parents, to continue guiding and training them, encouraging and loving them, as they face life's many challenges. These children are like the lovely rosebuds in the garden that delight our hearts with their beauty and fragrance. Our role as parents is to be the willing gardeners who carefully tend the roses and rejoice at the sight of their blossoming.

Like a flower that turns its face to meet the sun, so we train our children to turn toward God for sustenance. Like a leaf that curls itself to catch the rain, so we teach our children to drink from the spiritual spring. It is time, once again, to embark upon our journey, confident in the knowledge that we will attain our goal. With our children by our side, we continue on our way. Hand in hand, we walk this path together.

The Role of Parents

Parents play important roles at every stage of their children's lives. Their strong support, their loving guidance, and their tender affection provide the firm foundation on which children can grow and blossom. School-age children are wonderful blessings! Their joyful enthusiasm for life, their sincere appreciation for learning, and their warm and compassionate natures enrich our lives beyond compare. We learn from them even as they learn from us.

The school-age years are a time of intense learning for children—a time to work and to strive, a time to make new friends and relationships, and a time to experience life in all its beauty and complexities. For Bahá'í children, the school-age years are also a time of spiritual learning—a time to attain virtues and spiritual attributes, a time to study the history and principles of the Faith, and a time to develop a deep and abiding relationship with God.

Our challenge as Bahá'í parents is to raise children with strong spiritual values as well as strong Bahá'í identities in a world that has yet to understand us. I have always believed that my children would be better people and better prepared for life if they had a strong attachment to their Faith. I knew that if their hearts were connected to their Creator, they would be happier, more loving people. And I was confident that they would make the world a better place if they received a Bahá'í education.

When children reach the school-age years, parents take on new responsibilities. One of these is providing their children with a good education, one that will offer them the necessary skills for a successful life. Here we witness a unique aspect of the Bahá'í Faith. According to the Bahá'í writings, parents are entrusted with the sacred duty of educating their children in the arts and sciences as well as educating them spiritually.

As we study the writings, we come to understand that true education is a balance between the material and the spiritual. Bahá'í education, therefore, adopts a holistic approach, one that emphasizes the whole child, not just part. This means that we should take into account our children's mental, emotional, physical, and spiritual needs when we seek to educate them. Our consistent, loving efforts in these areas help our children to become happier, healthier, well-rounded individuals.

In this beautiful quote by 'Abdu'l-Bahá, fathers are encouraged to play prominent roles in both their children's spiritual and academic lives. He writes,

The father must always endeavour to educate his son and to acquaint him with the heavenly teachings. He must give him advice and exhort him at all times, teach him praiseworthy conduct and character, enable him to receive training at school and to be instructed in such arts and sciences as are deemed useful and necessary. In brief, let him instil into his mind the virtues and perfections of the world of humanity. Above all he should continually call to his mind the remembrance of God so that his throbbing veins and arteries may pulsate with the love of God.[1]

Mothers play important roles as well. In this beautiful passage from 'Abdu'l-Bahá, he describes the mother's role by using the gentle metaphor of the garden. He writes,

Let the mothers consider that whatever concerneth the education of children is of the first importance. Let them put forth every effort in this regard, for when the bough is green and tender it will grow in whatever way ye train it. Therefore is it incumbent upon the mothers to rear their little ones even as a gardener tendeth his young plants. Let them strive by day and by night to establish within their children faith and certitude, the fear of God, the love of the Beloved of the worlds, and all good qualities and traits.[2]

Mothers and fathers are special in the eyes of God. We have only to remember our own parents (or the parents we wish we had had) to understand the importance of parenting. Blessed are the parents who educate their children!

The Arts and Sciences

According to the Bahá'í Faith, the arts and sciences are of special importance. The arts and sciences encompass many different disciplines such as math, science, art, music, and literature. All of these disciplines constitute rich sources of knowledge for children to explore. We are fortunate that the Bahá'í writings contain a number of passages about the arts and sciences. By studying these passages, we can better guide our children in these areas.

In order to do this, we must first start at the beginning. 'Abdu'l-Bahá writes, *"As to the children: From the age of five their formal education must begin. That is, during the daytime they should be looked after in a place where there are teachers, and should learn good conduct."*[3] By the age of five, children have gained the necessary maturity to leave their families for the day and begin their academic training in a formal school setting. Here they begin the study of various subjects that are appropriate for their ages. In a Bahá'í-based curriculum, additional subjects would be studied, such as manners and the importance of spiritual virtues. Bahá'í-based curriculums serve to reinforce the values and belief system that are taught in the Bahá'í home.

It is a privilege for parents to experience learning through the eyes of a child. Everything we may have forgotten over the years—the excitement of learning to read for the first time, the deep sense of accomplishment when one masters a new skill, and the wonders of this incredibly diverse planet—all come rushing back to us with wonderful intensity. It is a fascinating time for parents and children, one filled with the wealth of new experiences.

In order to study the arts and sciences, children must first learn to read and write. Bahá'u'lláh states, *"It is incumbent upon the children to exert themselves to the utmost in acquiring the art of reading and writing. Writing skills that will provide for urgent needs will be enough for some; and then it is better and more fitting that they should spend their time in studying those branches of knowledge which are of use."*[4] The ability to read and write is important for all children. Reading opens up the world to them and writing offers them a powerful means of expression. Acquiring the art of reading and writing is essential to the goal of attaining knowledge.

Fathers are entrusted with a special role in this process. In the Kitáb-i-Aqdas, Bahá'u'lláh states, *"Unto every father hath been enjoined the instruction of his son and daughter in the art of reading and writing and in all that hath been laid down in the Holy Tablet."*[5] This role is entrusted to fathers to ensure that their children receive a proper education. This is also an honor for fathers, in much the same way as it is an honor for mothers to be the first educators of the child.

Both fathers and mothers are responsible for their children's education. This is a task of great significance and not one to be taken lightly. 'Abdu'l-Bahá assists us in this understanding when he writes, *"O ye who have peace of soul! Among the divine Texts as set forth in the Most Holy Book and also in other Tablets is this: it is incumbent upon the father and mother to train their children both in good conduct and the study of books; study, that is, to the degree required, so that no child, whether girl or boy, will remain illiterate."*[6]

The education of girls is of particular importance, especially when viewed in its spiritual context. In the notes to the Kitáb-i-Aqdas, we read the following: "'Abdu'l-Bahá, in His Tablets, not only calls attention to

92

the responsibility of parents to educate all their children, but He also clearly specifies that the *training and culture of daughters is more necessary than that of sons,* for girls will one day be mothers, and mothers are the first educators of the new generation. If it is not possible, therefore, for a family to educate all the children, preference is to be accorded to daughters since, through educated mothers, the benefits of knowledge can be most effectively and rapidly diffused throughout society."[7]

In Persia during the 1800s, the majority of people could neither read nor write. Bahá'u'lláh's declaration that all children should receive an education was revolutionary for its time and place. It is difficult for those of us living in modern societies and who take the education of girls and boys for granted to fully appreciate the importance of this extraordinary concept. 'Abdu'l-Bahá writes, *"Bahá'u'lláh hath proclaimed the universality of education, which is essential to the unity of mankind, that one and all may be equally educated, whether girls or boys, and receive the same education. When education is universalized in all schools, perfect communication between the members of the human race will be established. When all receive the same kind of education the foundations of war and contention will be utterly destroyed."*[8]

How important are the arts and sciences to the world of humanity? 'Abdu'l-Bahá states, *"Arts, crafts and sciences uplift the world of being, and are conducive to its exaltation."*[9] Children should be encouraged to study those arts, crafts, and sciences that exalt the individual and are of benefit to the society in which he lives. Bahá'u'lláh states, *"Of all the arts and sciences, set the children to studying those which will result in advantage to man, will ensure his progress and elevate his rank."*[10]

Children should also be encouraged to set high goals for themselves in both their material and spiritual lives. 'Abdu'l-Bahá instructs us in these goals. He writes, *"They must be constantly encouraged and made eager to gain all the summits of human accomplishment, so that from their earliest years they will be taught to have high aims, to conduct themselves well, to be chaste, pure, and undefiled, and will learn to be of powerful resolve and firm of purpose in all things. Let them not jest and trifle, but earnestly advance unto their goals, so that in every situation they will be found resolute and firm."*[11]

Children who grow up in stable, loving homes, who receive the proper material and spiritual training, and who have learned the value of being resolute and firm, are capable of accomplishing great things. 'Abdu'l-Bahá writes, *"The heart of 'Abdu'l-Bahá longeth, in its love, to find that Bahá'í young people, each and all, are known throughout the world for their intellectual attainments. There is no question but that they will exert all their efforts, their energies, their sense of pride, to acquire the sciences and arts."*[12]

We should remember to praise our children when they try their best and to be proud of them when they succeed in a goal. We should be supportive of their efforts and help them to remember that mistakes are also part of learning. Our task is not to burden our children or to expect more of them than they are able to accomplish. Instead, we should patiently and lovingly guide them to use all of their God-given talents to the best of their abilities and to learn how to strive for perfection. Striving for perfection is an important spiritual goal, as Bahá'u'lláh states, *"As for what the Supreme Pen hath previously set down, the reason is that in every art and skill, God loveth the highest perfection."*[13] It is in our gentle nurturing of our children's mental, emotional, and spiritual lives that we help them to attain their highest goals.

There are many ways we can assist our children in their school careers. We could help them with their homework and make learning a priority in the home. We could limit television and other distractions that are not worthy of their time. We could develop a relationship with their teachers and become involved in their schools. We could stimulate their imaginations with interesting stories and games. We could assist them with science projects or take them out to look at the stars. Our time and attention make all the difference in our children's lives. And we must believe in them, always believe in them, and help them to believe in themselves.

In his wonderful writings, 'Abdu'l-Bahá enlightens us as to the amazing potential in every child. He writes, *"O thou whose years are few, yet whose mental gifts are many! How many a child, though young in years, is yet mature and sound in judgment! How many an aged person is ignorant and confused! For growth and development depend on one's powers of intellect and reason, not on one's age or length of days."*[14] Helping our children to develop their powers of intellect and reason is important. Critical thinking allows them to combat superstition and to recognize truth. This is important in every area of life, not only in the arts and sciences.

We help our children learn how to think and to reason by talking with them about many different subjects. As children absorb all that the world has to offer, it is the parents who must help them to identify those things that lead to exaltation and those things that lead to abasement. As to the arts and sciences, we should expose them to what is good and dignified and true. We should also encourage investigation and discovery, and nurture their innate sense of wonder and curiosity about the world.

One of the most wonderful subjects that children can learn is music. Children enjoy singing songs and hearing beautiful music being played. In the Bahá'í Faith, music is encouraged. 'Abdu'l-Bahá offers us guidance on the role of music in children's lives. He states, *"The latent talents with which the hearts of these children are endowed will find expression through the medium of music. . . . It is incumbent upon each child to know something of music, for without knowledge of this art the melodies of instrument and voice cannot be rightly enjoyed. Likewise, it is necessary that the schools teach it in order that the souls and hearts of the pupils may become vivified and exhilarated and their lives be brightened with enjoyment."*[15]

Another activity that children enjoy is art. In young children, drawing and painting are spontaneous expressions of joy. This joy comes from the spiritual nature of art. It is a pleasure to watch children when they paint or sculpt or draw. It is evident that their hearts and minds are immersed in the experience and they exhibit a calmness and contentment not found in other activities. Children enjoy art because it nurtures their spirits and allows them to express themselves in a most profound way.

Why should we encourage our children to acquire the sciences and arts and what attitudes should we foster in them toward learning? The answers are closely connected to the love of God. 'Abdu'l-Bahá writes, *"Although to acquire the sciences and arts is the greatest glory of mankind, this is so only on condition that man's river flow into the mighty sea, and draw from God's ancient source His inspiration. When this cometh to pass, then every teacher is as a shoreless ocean, every pupil a prodigal fountain of knowledge. If, then, the pursuit of knowledge lead to the beauty of Him Who is the Object of all Knowledge, how excellent that goal; but if not, a mere drop will perhaps shut a man off from flooding grace, for with learning cometh arrogance and pride, and it bringeth on error and indifference to God."*[16]

Arrogance and pride do not bring us happiness no matter how knowledgeable we are or how many honors we may have received for that knowledge. As we all sadly know, knowledge taken to the extreme or knowledge that is completely separated from spiritual truth can even bring pain and destruction to the world. It is our understanding of the purpose of knowledge that makes learning of value to our lives. Knowledge should lead us to a greater understanding of the knowledge of God. And it is the knowledge of God that leads us to our purpose here on earth. Bahá'u'lláh states, *"True learning is that which is conducive to the well-being of the world, not to pride and self-conceit. . . ."*[17]

It is important to provide our children with the proper attitude for learning as well as a good education, one that is filled with study and striving and joy. To aid us in our efforts, 'Abdu'l-Bahá offers these encouraging words. He states, *"Among the greatest of all great services is the education of children, and promotion of the various sciences, crafts and arts. Praised be God, ye are now exerting strenuous efforts toward this end. The more ye persevere in this most important task, the more will ye witness the confirmations of God, to such a degree that ye yourselves will be astonished."*[18]

Work as Worship

This brings us to the wonderful principle of work as worship. In this new day, work done in the spirit of service is considered an act of worship. 'Abdu'l-Bahá offers these instructive words. He states,

"In the Bahá'í Cause arts, sciences and all crafts are (counted as) worship. The man who makes a piece of notepaper to the best of his ability, conscientiously, concentrating all his forces on perfecting it, is giving praise to God. Briefly, all effort and exertion put forth by man from the fullness of his heart is worship, if it is prompted by the highest motives and the will to do service to humanity."[19]

The world requires many different kinds of jobs for society to function properly. No matter what kinds of jobs people have, they can now be respected for serving the community in which they live. Building houses, growing crops, owning a business, learning a trade, or teaching in a school are all jobs that provide a service to the community. 'Abdu'l-Bahá states, *"All humanity must obtain a livelihood by sweat of the brow and bodily exertion, at the same time seeking to lift the burden of others, striving to be the source of comfort to souls and facilitating the means of living. This in itself is devotion to God."*[20]

When children learn the value of work as worship, they gain the spiritual incentive to work diligently in all that they do. Besides working to become proficient in their studies, they should also learn to help with household chores. Washing dishes, working in the garden, cleaning the house, and preparing the meals are all essential functions of the home that become opportunities for service. In fact, all members of the household should make it their duty to be of some service to the family.

I recall my neighbor's little boy who, at five years old, helped my husband build a fence. He showed up early one morning as my husband was pounding the nails. He must have heard the sound and become curious about the task. His request to help was enthusiastic and quite serious. He really did want to work. And so he ended up balancing the strips of wood that were placed horizontally across the posts so that my husband could hammer them in. What was at first mere kindness on my husband's part soon became genuine appreciation for this little fellow who wanted to be of some service to a friend. "He really did help me," my husband said afterward. We were both quite surprised about that.

Work builds self-confidence. It is said to build character as well. 'Abdu'l-Bahá encourages us to help our children learn perseverance and the ability to work and strive. He even advises us to accustom them to hardship, though hardship to some would not seem hardship to others, depending on where one lives in the world. No one else can give our children the feeling of satisfaction that a job well done can bring. Though some children are naturally industrious, others, unfortunately, are not. This requires parents to exhibit great amounts of patience and persistence to teach their children the value of work. Once learned, though, work provides great happiness. This is the gift that we give our children.

We may not have realized that raising children and educating them in the ways of God is also an act of worship. In my opinion, it is one of the best ways that we can thank God for His countless blessings, particularly for the blessing of our children. 'Abdu'l-Bahá, once again, offers us valuable words on raising children. He writes, *"Give them the advantage of every useful kind of knowledge. Let them share in every new and rare and wondrous craft and art. Bring them up to work and strive, and accustom them to hardship. Teach them to dedicate their lives to matters of great import, and inspire them to undertake studies that will benefit mankind.*"[21] As we put forth our sincere and tireless efforts to raise our children, may God bless us in this humble act of worship!

The Knowledge of God

Hidden within the hearts of all children is the longing desire to know their Creator. In order to teach our children about God, we must first acquire this knowledge for ourselves. It is helpful, therefore, to review some of the passages that further our knowledge of God. Bahá'u'lláh states, *"We have decreed, O people, that the highest and last end of all learning be the recognition of Him Who is the Object of all knowledge."*[22] When we believe in an All-Loving, All-Knowing Creator, we see the world with new eyes. Our minds are opened to new possibilities.

The more we study the writings, the more we comprehend that God is the Unknowable, the Unsearchable. Bahá'u'lláh states, *"Immeasurably exalted is He above the strivings of human mind to grasp His Essence, or of human tongue to describe His mystery."*[23] It is this understanding that allows us to be humble before God.

How, then, can we know God if He is the Unknowable, the Unsearchable? We know God through His Divine Manifestations, those holy and sanctified souls who manifest the attributes of God. Bahá'u'lláh states, *"The source of all learning is the knowledge of God, exalted be His glory, and this cannot be attained save through the knowledge of His Divine Manifestation."*[24]

In this day, God has bestowed upon humanity the precious blessing of Bahá'u'lláh. Through Him, God speaks to all mankind. Through Him, we are led to the knowledge of God. Bahá'u'lláh describes this sacred role. He states, *"Through the might of God and His power, and out of the treasury of His knowledge and wisdom, I have brought forth and revealed unto you the pearls that lay concealed in the depths of His everlasting ocean."*[25]

The Word of God is like a boundless ocean. If we stand on the shore of this ocean and look out over its great expanse, we are often overwhelmed by its immensity. But when we finally find the courage to dive in, we discover all manner of wonderful things. And soon we find that we are no longer thinking about the ocean or the impossibility of understanding it all. We are just enjoying our time there discovering all the treasures that lie hidden beneath the waves.

Should we not share these treasures with our children? Should we not dive in together and marvel at the wonder of them all? Should we not search for the pearls of great price? When we read the Bahá'í writings, even if only a few words a day, we educate our souls in the knowledge of God. The more we educate our own souls, the more we are able to educate our children's. Bahá'u'lláh, so beautifully, states, *"Immerse yourselves in the ocean of My words, that ye may unravel its secrets, and discover all the pearls of wisdom that lie hid in its depths."*[26]

Another way we can know God is through His magnificent creation. Bahá'u'lláh explains how God's creation leads us to the knowledge of God. He states, *"Every created thing in the whole universe is but a door leading into His knowledge, a sign of His sovereignty, a revelation of His names, a symbol of His majesty, a token of His power, a means of admittance into His straight Path. . . ."*[27]

Perhaps this is why we feel such peace when we sit in a lush green forest or lie by a sparkling stream. Perhaps this is why we feel such happiness when we gaze at the colors of flowers or smell their sweet fragrance in the air. Perhaps this is why we feel such awe when we fly over snow-capped mountains or such hope when rainbows appear after a storm. It is because every created thing is a sign of the knowledge of God, no matter how large or how small. Bahá'u'lláh states, *"From the exalted source, and out of the essence of His favor and bounty He hath entrusted every created thing with a sign of His knowledge. . . . This sign is the mirror of His beauty in the world of creation."*[28]

It is interesting what one remembers after all these years. I recall my sixth grade science class. Since we were studying the constellations, our teacher invited us, one evening, to look at the stars. I remember that the night was clear and crisp. We huddled together in our winter coats and peered up at the sky. How vast the canopy of stars God had placed above our heads—the moon, the stars, everything in perfect balance, suspended by the hand of God! It was not the constellations that impressed me that clear night, but the majesty of God's creation. I wonder how many of us, then, when we looked up at the sky, only saw the stars.

Let us educate our children by giving them precious memories of God's creation. Let us educate our children by giving them memories of the beauty of His sacred Word. How long will these memories last? Only God knows, but perhaps they will last forever. 'Abdu'l-Bahá encourages us to educate our children. He writes, *"Our meaning is that the friends must direct their attention toward the education and training of all the children . . . so that all of them, having, in the school of true learning, achieved the power of understanding and come to know the inner realities of the universe, will go on to uncover the signs and mysteries of God, and will find themselves illumined by the lights of the knowledge of the Lord, and by His love."*[29]

The Love of God

The beginning of all things is the love of God. We cannot speak about God without speaking of His love. The more we comprehend the nature of God's love, the more we can convey this love to our children. 'Abdu'l-Bahá writes, *"Know thou of a certainty that Love is the secret of God's holy Dispensation, the manifestation of the All-Merciful, the fountain of spiritual outpourings."*[30] Love is the reason for God's revelation to man.

'Abdu'l-Bahá instructs us in this spiritual truth. He states, *"Were it not for the love of God, the hearts would not be illumined. Were it not for the love of God, the pathway of the Kingdom would not be opened. Were it not for the love of God, the Holy Books would not have been revealed. Were it not for the love of God, the divine Prophets would not have been sent to the world. The foundation of all these bestowals is the love of God. Therefore, in the human world there is no greater power than the love of God."*[31]

Love plays a part in all of God's creation. Even the physical creation of the universe is dependent on the love of God. 'Abdu'l-Bahá writes, *"Love is the most great law that ruleth this mighty and heavenly cycle, the unique power that bindeth together the divers elements of this material world, the supreme magnetic force that directeth the movements of the spheres in the celestial realms."*[32] It is the love of God around which all creation circles.

How do we teach the love of God to children? We teach it gently, patiently, and lovingly. We teach it by taking them out to look at the stars. We teach it by praying with them and by talking with them and by sharing stories about Bahá'u'lláh. How do we teach the love of God to children? It is a smile, a kiss, a tear shed when prayers are said. It is singing the words of God with joy in our hearts. It is falling in love with the Words.

Teaching our children that God loves them is important. Helping them to learn to love God is also important. Bahá'u'lláh offers us this wise counsel. He states, *"O Son of Being! Love Me, that I may love thee. If thou lovest Me not, My love can in no wise reach thee. Know this, O servant."*[33] Loving God comes naturally to children when they are blessed with a spiritual education.

The most significant way that we can teach our children to be true Bahá'ís is through the love of God. I have always believed that if my children had a strong connection to their Faith, they would want to do what was right. I have always believed that if they saw themselves as spiritual beings, they would want to follow the straight path. I have always believed that if they felt joy when they read the writings, they would cherish them forever. I have always believed that if they loved God with all their hearts, they would honor Him all the days of their lives.

Bahá'u'lláh encourages us to love God. He states, *"O My servants! Deprive not yourselves of the unfading and resplendent Light that shineth within the Lamp of Divine glory. Let the flame of the love of God burn brightly within your radiant hearts. Feed it with the oil of Divine guidance, and protect it within the shelter of your constancy."*[34] May our children's hearts shine so brightly with the love of God that they will illuminate the whole earth!

Bahá'u'lláh educates us in the love of God. He states, *"Know thou that he is truly learned who hath acknowledged My Revelation, and drunk from the Ocean of My knowledge, and soared in the atmosphere of My love, and cast away all else besides Me, and taken firm hold on that which hath been sent down from the Kingdom of My wondrous utterance."*[35]

Teaching the Love of God: Stories of 'Abdu'l-Bahá

We are fortunate to have the perfect example set by 'Abdu'l-Bahá to teach us about the love of God. The following stories illustrate the gentle way in which 'Abdu'l-Bahá treated others. These stories are worthy of our time and attention if our goal is to be spiritual parents to our children.

In the spring of 1912, 'Abdu'l-Bahá visited the Bahá'ís in New York City. We are indebted to Howard Colby Ives for sharing his memories of that visit in his book *Portals to Freedom*. Although Howard Colby Ives was not a Bahá'í when he first met 'Abdu'l-Bahá, he became one a short time later and continued to love the Faith for the rest of his life. It was during a period of great personal and spiritual turmoil that Ives first met 'Abdu'l-Bahá. In this story, he describes one of those memorable meetings that took place in the Bahá'í home of Mr. and Mrs. Kinney. Ives writes,

In this home I had become a constant habitué. I could not keep away. One day 'Abdu'l-Bahá, the interpreter and I were alone in one of the smaller reception rooms on the ground floor. 'Abdu'l-Bahá had been speaking of some Christian doctrine and His interpretation of the words of Christ was so different from the accepted one that I could not restrain an expression of remonstrance. I remember speaking with some heat:

"How is it possible to be so sure?" I asked. "No one can say with certainty what Jesus meant after all these centuries of mis-interpretation and strife."

He intimated that it was quite possible.

It is indicative of my spiritual turmoil and my blindness to His station, that instead of His serenity and tone of authority impressing me as warranted it drove me to actual impatience. "That I cannot believe," I exclaimed.

I shall never forget the glance of outraged dignity the interpreter cast upon me. It was as though he would say: "Who are you to contradict or even to question 'Abdu'l-Bahá!"

But not so did 'Abdu'l-Bahá look at me. How I thank God that it was not! He looked at me a long moment before He spoke. His calm, beautiful eyes searched my soul with such love and understanding that all my momentary heat evaporated. He smiled as winningly as a lover smiles upon his beloved, and the arms of His spirit seemed to embrace me as He said softly that I should try my way and He would try His.

It was as though a cool hand had been laid upon a fevered brow; as though a cup of nectar had been held to parched lips; as though a key had unlocked my hard-bolted, crusted and rusted heart. The tears started and my voice trembled. "I'm sorry," I murmured.

Often since that day have I pondered on the tragic possibilities of the effect of an expression of the face. I have even thought I should like to write a book on The Glance that Saved the World, taking as a theme the way Jesus must have looked upon Peter after the three-fold denial. What could that glance have carried to the fear-stricken, doubting, angry Peter? Surely not the self-righteous, dignified look in the eyes of the interpreter for 'Abdu'l-Bahá. As surely it must have been something in the nature of the expression of all-embracing love, forgiveness and understanding with which 'Abdu'l-Bahá calmed and soothed and assured my heart.

. . .

Of one thing I am sure: upon that glance of 'Abdu'l-Bahá, upon that moment in which He turned upon me the searchlight of His inner being, hung my destiny throughout all the ages of immortal life.[36]

In another touching excerpt from this book, Ives describes the powerful emotions he felt when in the presence of 'Abdu'l-Bahá. He writes,

His lightest word, His slightest association with a soul was shot through with an illuminating radiance which lifted the hearer to a higher plane of consciousness. Our hearts burned within us when He spoke. And He never argued, of course. Nor did He press a point. He left one free. There was never an assumption of authority, rather He was ever the personification of humility. He taught "as if offering a gift to a king." He never told me what I should do, beyond suggesting that what I was doing was right. Nor did He ever tell me what I should believe. He made Truth and Love so beautiful and royal that my heart perforce did reverence. He showed me by His voice, manner, bearing, smile, how I should *be*, knowing that out of the pure soil of being the good fruit of deeds and words would surely spring.[37]

The last excerpt from this wonderful book describes a meeting between 'Abdu'l-Bahá and a clergyman who had requested an interview with him for an article he was writing. It seems that the clergyman talked on and on, asking 'Abdu'l-Bahá many long and hypothetical questions. Ives started to grow impatient and questioned the man's motives. But not so did 'Abdu'l-Baha. Ives writes, "He looked at the interviewer with that indescribable expression of understanding love which never failed His face was radiant with an inner flame." When finally the interviewer paused, 'Abdu'l-Bahá began to speak to him about the love of God. Ives writes,

Within five minutes His questioner had become humble, for the moment, at least, a disciple at His feet. He seemed to have been transported to another world, as indeed we all were. His face shone faintly as though he had received an inner illumination. Then 'Abdu'l-Bahá rose. We all rose with Him in body as we had risen with Him in spirit. He lovingly embraced the doctor and led him towards the door. At the threshold He paused. His eyes had lighted upon a large bunch of American Beauty roses which one of the friends had brought to Him that morning. There were at least two dozen of them, perhaps three. There were so many and their stems so long that they had been placed in an earthenware umbrella stand. We all had noticed their beauty and fragrance.

No sooner had 'Abdu'l-Bahá's eyes lighted upon them than He laughed aloud; His boyish hearty laughter rang through the room. He stooped, gathered the whole bunch in His arms, straightened and placed them all in the arms of His visitor. Never shall I forget that round, bespectacled, grey head above that immense bunch of lovely flowers. So surprised, so radiant, so humble, so transformed. Ah! 'Abdu'l-Bahá knew how to teach the Love of God![38]

The Importance of Prayer

These lovely stories lead us to the subject of prayer. What is prayer? Prayer is like the cool summer shower that waters the thirsty plants. Prayer is like the sun's bright rays that gently warm the flowers. Just as tiny rosebuds need water and light in order to blossom, children need prayer in order to grow. The life of the soul is nurtured through prayer.

When children say prayers in the morning, their souls are inspired with spiritually uplifting words to guide them throughout the day. When children say prayers at night, their souls are strengthened with comforting, heavenly words as they sleep. 'Abdu'l-Bahá encourages us to pray. He writes, *"Praise be to God, thy heart is engaged in the commemoration of God, thy soul is gladdened by the glad tidings of God and thou art absorbed in prayer. The state of prayer is the best of conditions, for man is then associating with God. Prayer verily bestoweth life, particularly when offered in private and at times, such as midnight, when freed from daily cares."*[39]

What prayers are most acceptable to God? The Báb offers us this guidance. He writes, *"The most acceptable prayer is the one offered with the utmost spirituality and radiance; its prolongation hath not been and is not beloved by God. The more detached and the purer the prayer, the more acceptable is it in the presence of God."*[40] We understand from this passage that long hours in prayer may not be necessary. What seems to be most important is the quality of our prayers, our detachment from the world, and our attitude of humbleness and devotion.

It is important to teach our children how to pray and how to appreciate the sacredness of prayer. It is also important to pray *with* our children and to make them feel valued and loved. When children experience prayer in a loving way, they will want to continue it for the rest of their lives. The act of praying together nurtures the hearts of children and strengthens the family bond. I believe that the single, most significant, act that connected my sons' hearts to God was consistent, loving prayer.

My husband and I learned about prayer from some of the first Bahá'ís we met. They were much older than we were, and their gentle eyes taught us many things. They recited prayers with the utmost dignity and respect. At times, they became so overwhelmed by the beauty of the words that their eyes would fill with tears and they would not be able to continue. Our Persian Bahá'í friends also taught us about prayer. During prayers, they sat upright, but relaxed, in their chairs. Their attitudes were peaceful, respectful, and focused. As they chanted the prayers in Persian, they closed their eyes and seemed to float away. Their children exhibited a special radiance. We are thankful for these dear friends who taught us about the sacredness of prayer.

Sometimes we learn about prayer through stories. The following story offers us a glimpse into the unique way 'Abdu'l-Bahá taught the meaning of prayer.

'When 'Abdu'l-Bahá was in New York, He called to Him an ardent Bahá'í and said, "If you will come to Me at dawn tomorrow, I will teach you to pray."

Delighted, Mr M arose at four and crossed the city, arriving for his lesson at six. With what exultant expectation he must have greeted this opportunity! He found 'Abdu'l-Bahá already at prayer, kneeling by the side of the bed. Mr M followed suit, taking care to place himself directly across.

'Seeing that 'Abdu'l-Bahá was quite lost in His Own reverie, Mr M began to pray silently for his friends, his family and finally for the crowned heads of Europe. No word was uttered by the quiet Man before him. He went over all the prayers he knew then, and repeated them twice, three times—still no sound broke the expectant hush.

'Mr M surreptitiously rubbed one knee and wondered vaguely about his back. He began again, hearing as he did so, the birds heralding the dawn outside the window. An hour passed, and finally two. Mr M was quite numb now. His eyes, roving along the wall, caught sight of a large crack. He dallied with a touch of indignation but let his gaze pass again to the still figure across the bed.

'The ecstasy that he saw arrested him and he drank deeply of the sight. Suddenly he wanted to pray like that. Selfish desires were forgotten. Sorrow, conflict, and even his immediate surroundings were as if they had never been. He was conscious of only one thing, a passionate desire to draw near to God.

'Closing his eyes again he set the world firmly aside, and amazingly his heart teemed with prayer, eager, joyous, tumultuous prayer. He felt cleansed by humility and lifted by a new peace. 'Abdu'l-Bahá had taught him to pray!

'The "Master of 'Akká" immediately arose and came to him. His eyes rested smilingly upon the newly humbled Mr M. "When you pray," He said, "you must not think of your aching body, nor of the birds outside the window, nor of the cracks in the wall!"

'He became very serious then, and added, "When you wish to pray you must first know that you are standing in the presence of the Almighty!"'[41]

How fortunate are we to have such special stories! How fortunate are we to have such special prayers! Let us not forget to pray *for* our children or to teach them the value of prayer. Soon time will pass and, before we know it, our children will be saying sweet prayers for their parents.

Study, Memorization, and Recitation

Study of the Creative Word is essential to the goal of attaining knowledge. Bahá'u'lláh states, *"Teach ye your children so that they may peruse the divine verses every morn and eve."*[42] To *"peruse"* means "to read with thoroughness and care." Reading and studying the Word of God on a daily basis helps our children to discover all of the gems of knowledge that are contained therein.

Study of the Creative Word need not be complicated or time-consuming. It can be as simple as reading one verse with our children in the morning before they go to school and one verse in the evening before they go to sleep at night. Bahá'u'lláh states, *"To read but one of the verses of My Revelation is better than to peruse the Scriptures of both the former and latter generations. This is the Utterance of the*

All-Merciful, would that ye had ears to hear! Say: This is the essence of knowledge, did ye but understand."[43]

With what attitudes should we read the Word of God? Bahá'u'lláh states, *"The prime requisite is the eagerness and love of sanctified souls to read the Word of God. To read one verse, or even one word, in a spirit of joy and radiance, is preferable to the perusal of many Books."*[44] Study of the Creative Word should never be a chore for children nor should the writings be so overemphasized that they become tiresome. Reading the Bahá'í writings should be like visiting a beautiful garden, one where we are refreshed, enlightened, and inspired. Like precious jewels in a mine that must be discovered or pearls hidden in the depths of the sea, so can the writings be, if children's ages, abilities, and willingness to learn are respected.

One of the ways that children enjoy learning is by memorization. Shoghi Effendi writes, *"The Master used to attach much importance to the learning by heart of the Tablets of Bahá'u'lláh and the Báb. During His days it was a usual work of the children of the household to learn Tablets by heart. . . . The practice is most useful to implant the ideas and spirit those words contain into the minds of children."*[45] Memorization of the Hidden Words and of special prayers is a good place to start for children. The Hidden Words also provides a valuable source of knowledge since within it lies the inner essence of all religions.

When my sons were quite young, they took Spanish lessons from their kindergarten teacher. She told me that if children learned a little Spanish when they were young, they would learn it more quickly when they were older. It seems that the brain receives the information and then stores it away for further use. The soul, also, receives spiritual knowledge through study and prayer. Years later, the soul will draw from that prayer, that quote, that memory, when it is needed most. The soul remembers.

Along with memorization comes recitation. Bahá'u'lláh encourages children to recite the sacred words. He states, *"Teach unto your children the words that have been sent down from God, that they may recite them in the sweetest of tones. This standeth revealed in a mighty Book."*[46] Children seem to enjoy memorization and recitation, particularly of the Creative Word. Even children who are not Bahá'ís seem to enjoy this activity. In both cases, I believe that their hearts are touched by the sweet sound of their voices reciting these beautiful words.

Bahá'u'lláh also encourages children to recite the sacred words in the Bahá'í Houses of Worship throughout the world. He states, *"Teach your children the verses revealed from the heaven of majesty and power, so that, in most melodious tones, they may recite the Tablets of the All-Merciful in the alcoves within the Mashriqu'l-Adhkárs. Whoever hath been transported by the rapture born of adoration for My Name, the Most Compassionate, will recite the verses of God in such wise as to captivate the hearts of those yet wrapped in slumber."*[47]

In her wonderful book *The Priceless Pearl*, Rúhíyyih Rabbani shares with us another touching story about Shoghi Effendi as a young child. This sweet story was told to her by Dr. Zia Baghdadi, a close friend of the family. She writes,

Dr. Baghdadi states that when Shoghi Effendi was only five years old he was pestering the Master to write something for him, whereupon 'Abdu'l-Bahá wrote this touching and revealing letter in His own hand:

He is God!

O My Shoghi, I have no time to talk, leave me alone! You said "write"—I have written. What else should be done? Now is not the time for you to read and write, it is the time for jumping about and chanting "O my God!", therefore memorize the prayers of the Blessed Beauty and chant them that I may hear them, because there is no time for anything else.

It seems that when this wonderful gift reached the child he set himself to memorize a number of Bahá'u'lláh's prayers and would chant them so loudly that the entire neighbourhood could hear his voice; when his parents and other members of the Master's family remonstrated with him, Shoghi Effendi replied, according to Dr. Baghdadi, "The Master wrote to me to chant that He may hear me! I am doing my best!" and he kept on chanting at the top of his voice for many hours every day. Finally his parents begged the Master to stop him, but He told them to let Shoghi Effendi alone. This was one aspect of the small boy's chanting. We are told there was another: he had memorized some touching passages written by 'Abdu'l-Bahá after the Ascension of Bahá'u'lláh and when he chanted these the tears would roll down the earnest little face. From another source we are told that when the Master was requested by a western friend, at that time living in His home, to reveal a prayer for children He did so, and the first to memorize it and chant it was Shoghi Effendi who would also chant it in the meetings of the friends.[48]

These beautiful prayers and writings touched the heart and mind of Shoghi Effendi as a young boy and contributed greatly to the man he would become. Our dear Shoghi Effendi! May God bless him for all eternity!

Eloquent Speech

Speech is a special blessing bestowed upon human beings by their Creator. Through the power of speech, we communicate with others. Through the power of speech, we share who we are with the world. Just as we encourage our children to do well in school, to study the writings, and to memorize and recite the sacred verses, so should we encourage them to develop their powers of eloquent speech.

In order to be courteous and mannerly, children must be patiently trained by their parents. In like manner, children must be patiently trained to properly and effectively communicate. This communication greatly influences the way that they are perceived by others and, in a large part, influences the way that they perceive themselves. Just as our standards should be high in terms of our academic achievements, so should our standards be high in terms of our manners, behavior, and speech. Children should be trained to speak clearly, to stand up straight when they speak, and to hold their heads with dignity. When children speak with dignity and eloquence, they face the world in a more confident manner.

One of the reasons we should train our children to speak with eloquence is to enable them to give speeches in the future. 'Abdu'l-Bahá writes, *"Encourage ye the school children, from their earliest years, to deliver speeches of high quality, so that in their leisure time they will engage in giving cogent and effective talks, expressing themselves with clarity and eloquence."*[49] One of the ways that we can help our children to develop these impressive skills is by talking with them about many different subjects and by encouraging them to express themselves freely.

Bahá'í children are also encouraged to share their knowledge of the Bahá'í Faith. In a letter written on behalf of Shoghi Effendi to an individual, we read the following: *"Shoghi Effendi was very interested to hear of the plans you are making for the education of your children. He hopes that they will all grow to be ardent adherents of the Bahá'í Cause, able servants of the Blessed Threshold, and eloquent speakers on religious and social subjects."*[50] A good way for children to learn to speak about the Faith is by sharing stories about Bahá'u'lláh or 'Abdu'l-Bahá. Storytelling is a wonderful art form. As with all art forms, practice is necessary. We should encourage our children to become devoted speakers of the Faith so that they can share its healing message with the world.

Communicating with others on a daily basis is also an important aspect of speech. We should be kind to others in the way that we speak with them, and also in the way that we speak about them. We should always think before we speak and consider how our words will fall on others. Kindness and courtesy are called for in every situation, whether we are speaking with our friends and acquaintances, or we are speaking with our children. Here again, children learn by example. How we speak to people, the sound of our voice, our kindness or unkindness as well as our willingness to refrain from backbiting, sets the standard for all of our children's future communications with others.

Another important aspect of speech is truthfulness. Although truthfulness is a spiritual quality, it manifests itself through speech.

Bahá'u'lláh states, *"Beautify your tongues, O people, with truthfulness, and adorn your souls with the ornament of honesty."*[51] Truthfulness is an important quality if one hopes to possess a good character. Let us train our children to be honest and truthful, tactful and wise, courteous and kind, and to speak with eloquence and refinement. In this way, will we help them shine their light upon the world!

Divine Virtues

The attainment of divine virtues is a great blessing. 'Abdu'l-Bahá states, *"The greatest bestowal of God to man is the capacity to attain human virtues."*[52] What are human virtues? Human virtues are spiritual qualities such as kindness, forgiveness, generosity, truthfulness, and patience. Why are these virtues important? 'Abdu'l-Bahá writes, *"It is religion . . . which produces all human virtues, and it is these virtues which are the bright candles of civilization."*[53]

Where do children first learn virtues? When they are young, children first learn virtues from their mothers. 'Abdu'l-Bahá describes this sacred role. He writes, *"Mothers are the first educators of children, who establish virtues in the child's inner nature. They encourage the child to acquire perfections and goodly manners, warn him against unbecoming qualities, and encourage him to show forth resolve, firmness, and endurance under hardship, and to advance on the high road to progress."*[54] Mothers are important because they gently and lovingly train their children in the ways of God.

The training of children requires the consistent and loving efforts of both parents. Parents train their children through countless examples and gentle reminders that take place over a long period of time. 'Abdu'l-Bahá tells us that training children to acquire virtues is even more important than educating them in the study of books. He writes,

> *Training in morals and good conduct is far more important than book learning. A child that is cleanly, agreeable, of good character, well-behaved—even though he be ignorant—is preferable to a child that is rude, unwashed, ill-natured, and yet becoming deeply versed in all the sciences and arts. The reason for this is that the child who conducts himself well, even though he be ignorant, is of benefit to others, while an ill-natured, ill-behaved child is corrupted and harmful to others, even though he be learned. If, however, the child be trained to be both learned and good, the result is light upon light.*[55]

Through the beautiful and descriptive language of the writings, we expand our minds and hearts to embrace new spiritual concepts. The image of *"light upon light"* resembles, in many ways, the concept of angels found in various cultures. Angels are portrayed as heavenly beings who are endowed with light and are believed to be spiritually enlightened souls who exist in the next world. Surely, spiritually enlightened souls can also exist in this world and would be identified as those who are illumined with the light of divine virtues.

During his lifetime, many people wrote to 'Abdu'l-Bahá about the education and training of children. In their struggles to understand the new Faith they had embraced, 'Abdu'l-Bahá offered them loving words of guidance. To an individual, he replied,

O thou who gazeth upon the Kingdom of God! Thy letter was received and we note that thou art engaged in teaching the children of the believers, that these tender little ones have been learning The Hidden Words and the prayers and what it meaneth to be a Bahá'í.

The instruction of these children is even as the work of a loving gardener who tendeth his young plants in the flowerings fields of the All-Glorious. There is no doubt that it will yield the desired results; especially is this true of instruction as to Bahá'í obligations and Bahá'í conduct, for the little children must needs be made aware in their very heart and soul that "Bahá'í" is not just a name but a truth. Every child must be trained in the things of the spirit, so that he may embody all the virtues and become a source of glory to the Cause of God. Otherwise, the mere word "Bahá'í," if it yield no fruit, will come to nothing.

Strive then to the best of thine ability to let these children know that a Bahá'í is one who embodieth all the perfections, that he must shine out like a lighted taper—not be darkness upon darkness and yet bear the name "Bahá'í."[56]

Through consistent and loving training, our children will grow stronger with each day, they will become endowed with the brightness of many virtues, and they will grow straight and tall as young plants. 'Abdu'l-Bahá encourages us to train our children. He writes, *"A child is as a young plant: it will grow in whatever way you train it. If you rear it to be truthful, and kind, and righteous, it will grow straight, it will be fresh and tender, and will flourish."*[57]

Character

Character is an important spiritual attribute and one that is mentioned numerous times in the writings. To possess a good character means to exhibit such praiseworthy qualities as honor, integrity, moral strength, honesty, goodness, uprightness, and fortitude. Years ago, if someone said, "He is a man of character" or "She is a woman of character," it would be one of the highest compliments that a person could receive. We do not hear much about character these days, but that does not lessen its importance. 'Abdu'l-Bahá writes, *"Ye should consider the question of goodly character as of the first importance. It is incumbent upon every father and mother to counsel their children over a long period, and guide them unto those things which lead to everlasting honor."*[58]

Once again, mothers play important roles in this process. 'Abdu'l-Bahá states, *"The mother is the first teacher of the child. For children, at the beginning of life, are fresh and tender as a young twig, and can be trained in any fashion you desire. If you rear the child to be straight, he will grow straight, in perfect symmetry. It is clear that the mother is the first teacher and that it is she who establisheth the character and conduct of the child."*[59]

At what age should children learn good character? 'Abdu'l-Bahá writes, *"It is extremely difficult to teach the individual and refine his character once puberty is passed. By then, as experience hath shown, even if every effort be exerted to modify some tendency of his, it all availeth nothing. He may, perhaps, improve somewhat today; but let a few days pass and he forgetteth, and turneth backward to his habitual condition and accustomed ways. Therefore it is in the early childhood that a firm foundation must be laid. While the branch is green and tender it can easily be made straight."*[60] All things taught in early childhood have a great effect. Since young children are innocent and pure, they embrace these spiritual concepts more readily and a deeper impression is made upon their tender souls.

One of the ways that we can help our children learn good character is by educating them about the difference between right and wrong. Without this vital training, they wander, helpless, in the darkness of ignorance and despair. 'Abdu'l-Bahá writes, *"The root cause of wrongdoing is ignorance, and we must therefore hold fast to the tools of perception and knowledge. Good character must be taught. Light must be spread afar, so that, in the school of humanity, all may acquire the heavenly characteristics of the spirit. . . ."*[61] Here again, we observe that *"light"* is mentioned. When we follow the laws of God, we learn to acquire good characters and our souls are filled with a heavenly light.

Our own characters, in a large part, determine the characters of our children. In order to help our children learn good character, we must first strive willingly to purify our own. 'Abdu'l-Bahá states, *"The most vital duty, in this day, is to purify your characters, to correct your manners, and improve your conduct. The beloved of the Merciful must show forth such character and conduct among His creatures, that the fragrance of their holiness may be shed upon the whole world, and may quicken the dead, inasmuch as the purpose of the Manifestation of God and the dawning of the limitless lights of the Invisible is to educate the souls of men, and refine the character of every living man. . . ."*[62]

A school principal once told me of a conversation she had with a teacher who she was interviewing for a job. The principal asked the teacher, "How do you maintain order in the classroom? How do you keep the children's attention and respect? In short, how do you hold the children?" The teacher thought for a moment and then said confidently, "I hold them with the strength of my character." Every teacher knows that what she said is true. Character implies an inner strength, one that people recognize and respond to. It is the strength of positive intentions, along with the will to do what is right. In the case of the teacher, she knew what was necessary in order to properly educate the children in her classroom. Discipline, order, and strength were required. Commitment, dedication, and resolve were called for. Certainly, parents need this same kind of inner strength to raise their children to be mentally, physically, and spiritually strong. "Strength of character" is a phrase worth pondering.

It is a fact of life that we grow through tests. Just as metal is purified through fire so is character refined through the many challenges and changes of life. Character is a learned attribute, but it is also earned. The teacher would not know that she could "hold" her class through her strength of character had she not been challenged to do so. She would not have needed to develop this quality if life were easy and all the children acted perfectly in her class.

As we refine our characters, we move closer to our spiritual potential. How important is good character? Bahá'u'lláh offers us these potent words. He states, *"A good character is, verily, the best mantle for men from God. With it He adorneth the temples of His loved ones. By My life! The light of a good character surpasseth the light of the sun and the radiance thereof. Whoso attaineth unto it is accounted as a jewel among men. The glory and the upliftment of the world must needs depend upon it. A goodly character is a means whereby men are guided to the Straight Path and are led to the Great Announcement. Well is it with him who is adorned with the saintly attributes and character of the Concourse on High.*"[63]

The training of children in good character is an important and honorable endeavor for parents. Character is the gift that we give our children when we train them in the ways of God. 'Abdu'l-Bahá writes, *"The purport is this, that to train the character of humankind is one of the weightiest commandments of God, and the influence of such training is the same as that which the sun exerteth over tree and fruit. Children must be most carefully watched over, protected and trained; in such consisteth true parenthood and parental mercy."*[64] He also writes, *"Wherefore doth every child, new-risen in the garden of Heavenly love, require the utmost training and care."*[65]

Excellence and Refinement

Excellence and refinement are important spiritual qualities that should distinguish our dear children. Children should be encouraged to strive for excellence in every area of their lives, both in their spiritual qualities and in their academic achievements. 'Abdu'l-Bahá states, *"Take the utmost care to give them high ideals and goals, so that once they come of age, they will cast their beams like brilliant candles on the world, and . . . will set their hearts on achieving everlasting honor and acquiring all the excellences of humankind."*[66] When we encourage our children to strive for excellence, they discover all the talents and capacities that lie latent within.

Children should also be distinguished by their refinement. Refinement is described in such terms as tastefulness, grace, cultivation, and dignity. Manners and politeness are a part of refinement. Eloquent speech is a part of refinement. In whatever way it is used, refinement requires us to raise ourselves to a higher standard and to free ourselves from unworthy habits and behaviors. To further understand the term *"refinement,"* we look to the meaning of "refine." To "refine" means "to bring to a *purer* state," as oil is refined by separating it from its impurities. To "refine" also means "to bring to a *finer* state," as gems are refined through polishing.

In the Kitáb-i-Aqdas, Bahá'u'lláh states, *"Adopt ye such usages as are most in keeping with refinement. He, verily, desireth to see in you the manners of the inmates of Paradise in His mighty and most sublime Kingdom."*[67] A note from the Kitáb-i-Aqdas helps to explain this passage. It states, "This is the first of several passages referring to the importance of refinement and cleanliness. The original Arabic word 'laṭáfah' rendered here as *'refinement,'* has a wide range of meanings with both spiritual and physical implications, such as elegance, gracefulness, cleanliness, civility, politeness, gentleness, delicacy and graciousness, as well as being subtle, refined, sanctified and pure."[68]

Refinement can also be thought of as a heightened sensibility to all that is good and beautiful. 'Abdu'l-Bahá states, *"It is natural for the heart and spirit to take pleasure and enjoyment in all things that show forth symmetry, harmony, and perfection. For instance: a beautiful house, a well designed garden, a symmetrical line, a graceful motion, a well written book, pleasing garments—in fact, all things that have in themselves grace or beauty are pleasing to the heart and spirit. . . ."*[69]

How does refinement influence our spiritual development? *"My meaning is this,"* states 'Abdu'l-Bahá, *"that in every aspect of life, purity and holiness, cleanliness and refinement, exalt the human condition and further the development of man's inner reality."*[70] As we help our children improve their manners, strive for excellence, and rise to new standards of cleanliness and refinement, we nurture their spirits and they become more of the people who they were meant to be.

One of the individuals who best combined the qualities of excellence and refinement was Louis Gregory. Louis Gregory was born the son of slaves in South Carolina in 1874. When he grew up, he became a lawyer and was one of the first people to become a Bahá'í during the earliest days of the Faith in the United States. Because of his sincere devotion and love for the Faith, he traveled extensively to share its teachings. His emphasis on excellence and refinement enabled him to share his Faith in the best possible way. From the inspiring book *To Move The World*, a biography about his life, we read the following:

> Although his poverty was real, he did not advertise it. On the contrary, he paid careful attention to his appearance. . . . He was conscious of his role as a representative of the Bahá'í Faith and of the importance of looking his best, according to the standards of the time. His training as a tailor enabled him to maintain his well-groomed appearance even during long months of travel. Roy Williams, a friend and associate for many years, has observed that by careful brushing and pressing Louis Gregory made the most of even one suit; he always looked distinguished and created a favorable impression.[71]

And, in another part of the book, we read,

The powerful impression that Louis Gregory made, so strong that it could bring a white audience to its feet, is still apparent in recollections shared almost thirty years after his passing by those who knew him. They describe him graphically, as if he had just left the room. He was tall, they tell us, perhaps only about six feet but appearing taller because of his unusually erect carriage. When he spoke, he looked people in the eye, his contemporaries say; and his beautiful, deep voice held their attention. In public lectures he quoted and paraphrased extensively from the Bahá'í writings, so that if his listeners closed their eyes they might have thought the words were 'Abdu'l-Bahá's own. The effect of Mr. Gregory's stately bearing was enhanced by his immaculate grooming and his great courtesy. He was, indeed, courtly in manner, but with no affectation. At the same time he was invariably humble, without any trace of an excessive modesty that calls attention to itself. In personal conversation his eyes sparkled, and his smile was always ready. . . .[72]

Louis Gregory and other outstanding Bahá'ís from the early days of the Faith serve as spiritual examples for us all. They were, in their passionate desire to serve their Faith, ordinary people who did extraordinary things. Let us honor their examples by raising the standards of our speech, our graciousness, and our dignity, and helping our children to do the same. In this way, will all people know that these lovely children are those who manifest the qualities of the spirit!

Love and Compassion

The Bahá'í Faith is, first and foremost, a religion of love. Love for humanity and the unity of the human race are two important principles of the Bahá'í Faith. Bahá'u'lláh states, *"The Great Being saith: O ye children of men! The fundamental purpose animating the Faith of God and His Religion is to safeguard the interests and promote the unity of the human race, and to foster the spirit of love and fellowship amongst men."*[73] This principle of love for humanity was what attracted me to the Bahá'í Faith many years ago. My husband and I realized, at that time, that we had found a Faith we could wholeheartedly embrace and we vowed to raise our children as Bahá'ís.

The Bahá'í Faith teaches us that we are all children of one God and all members of one family. Children who are raised with these wonderful principles celebrate the beauty of diversity and acknowledge their connection to every human being. They also possess an openness of heart that embraces all peoples and cultures, and allows them to see the face of God in every person. Bahá'u'lláh states, *"Let your vision be world-embracing, rather than confined to your own self."*[74] What a remarkable gift we give our children—a world-embracing vision that inspires them to feel love and compassion for their brothers and sisters around the world!

In a difficult world, it is not always easy to love others. 'Abdu'l-Bahá offers these wise words of advice. He states, *"Love the creatures for the sake of God and not for themselves. You will never become angry or impatient if you love them for the sake of God. Humanity is not perfect. There are imperfections in every human being, and you will always become unhappy if you look toward the people themselves. But if you look toward God, you will love them and be kind to them, for the world of God is the world of perfection and complete mercy.*"[75]

The love and compassion that we feel for humanity should also apply to our relationships within the Bahá'í community. In a letter written on behalf of Shoghi Effendi, we read the following: *"The friends must be patient with each other. . . .The greater the patience, the loving understanding and the forbearance the believers show towards each other and their shortcomings, the greater will be the progress of the whole Bahá'í community at large.*"[76]

The love and compassion that children experience in their Bahá'í communities greatly influences their Bahá'í identities. When my older son was six years old, our community was extremely small, and there were only two other Bahá'í children, one of whom was my two-year-old son. I knew it was important for my elder son to have a Bahá'í friend his own age, so I began praying fervently to God to give him just one friend. I prayed and I prayed, but nothing seemed to happen.

It was about a year later that a new Bahá'í family moved into our community. They had no sons, but they did have two wonderful teenage daughters. Right from the start, these girls treated my sons as if they were their beloved little brothers. They gave them much love and attention by kissing them and hugging them, by talking with them, and by playing with them. Their parents were warm and affectionate as well. Their father talked with them and laughed with them. Their mother spoke lovingly to them and cooked good food for them to eat. Feasts were happy occasions filled with warm feelings, spiritual nourishment, and wonderful food. My sons looked forward to going to Feasts and Holy Days to see their new Bahá'í friends. I soon realized that even though God did not give me exactly what I had prayed for, He gave us something better instead. He gave us people who loved us and that made all the difference.

How can we foster a spirit of love and compassion in the Bahá'í community? Besides participating in Bahá'í functions, we could plan fun activities as well. Having Bahá'ís over for dinner, going on picnics together, or even camping out are ways that Bahá'í families can get to know each other better. Creating bonds of love and friendship within the Bahá'í community is extremely important, especially for the children. All people, no matter what age they may be, long for a sense of community and a sense of belonging. Praying together, playing together, laughing together, and talking together are ways that we can nurture a strong Bahá'í community.

Children learn much about the value of love and compassion within marriage from their parents. The power of example goes far beyond words. When mothers and fathers treat each other with love and respect, with dignity and compassion, and with patience and courtesy, their children learn what it means to be a loving couple. Love begins in the home. We cannot teach our children about the Bahá'í principle of the equality of men and women unless they see its loving example in the home. The true Bahá'í marriage is one where love and tenderness are always present and where kindness and compassion are expressed through word and deed.

'Abdu'l-Bahá offers us a vision of a loving couple when he states,

In this glorious Cause the life of a married couple should resemble the life of the angels in heaven—a life full of joy and spiritual delight, a life of unity and concord, a friendship both mental and

physical. The home should be orderly and well-organized. Their ideas and thoughts should be like the rays of the sun of truth and the radiance of the brilliant stars in the heavens. Even as two birds they should warble melodies upon the branches of the tree of fellowship and harmony. They should always be elated with joy and gladness and be a source of happiness to the hearts of others. They should set an example to their fellowmen, manifest true and sincere love towards each other and educate their children in such a manner as to blazon the fame and glory of their family.[77]

Teaching our children to feel love and compassion towards others also extends to their relationship to future generations. Children should learn to love and to protect the earth on which they stand—its plants and animals, its clouds and trees, and everything that God created. We are connected to the earth even as we are connected to each other. 'Abdu'l-Bahá describes this mysterious connection when he writes, *"Reflect upon the inner realities of the universe, the secret wisdoms involved, the enigmas, the interrelationships, the rules that govern all. For every part of the universe is connected with every other part by ties that are very powerful and admit of no imbalance, nor any slackening whatever."*[78] In what ways can we teach our children to love, respect, and protect their environment? In what ways can we teach our children to love, respect, and protect each other? Questions such as these require time for reflection. Our children's attitudes toward the earth, their parents, and other people will influence every action they will take for the rest of their lives.

Let us train our children to show forth love and compassion toward others, to feel a sense of responsibility to the world, to promote the equality of men and women, and to banish all forms of hatred and prejudice. 'Abdu'l-Bahá offers us these inspiring words. He states,

> *O peoples of the world! The Sun of Truth hath risen to illumine the whole earth, and to spiritualize the community of man. Laudable are the results and the fruits thereof, abundant the holy evidences deriving from this grace. This is mercy unalloyed and purest bounty; it is light for the world and all its peoples; it is harmony and fellowship, and love and solidarity; indeed it is compassion and unity, and the end of foreignness; it is the being at one, in complete dignity and freedom, with all on earth.*[79]

Developing a Bahá'í Identity

Developing a strong Bahá'í identity is important for all Bahá'í children. As parents, we want our children to feel close to the Faith, to enjoy Bahá'í functions, and to love Bahá'u'lláh and 'Abdu'l-Bahá. In my experience, children's Bahá'í identities are influenced by two important factors: their parents and positive Bahá'í experiences.

Parents first strengthen their children's Bahá'í identities through love and affection, through prayer and reverence, and through training and education. Because children so strongly identify with their mothers, their mothers serve as the primary influences in their Bahá'í identities. It is important, therefore, for mothers to be strong in the Faith and to be deeply committed to the spiritual education of their children. 'Abdu'l-Bahá states, *"Consider that if the mother is a believer, the children will become believers too, even if the father denieth the Faith; while, if the mother is not a believer, the children are deprived of faith, even if the father be a believer convinced and firm. Such is the usual outcome, except in rare cases."*[80]

This is not to say that the father's role is unimportant. Fathers are extremely important in the formation of their children's Bahá'í identities, particularly when their children get older. Parents who love the Faith and who have a close connection to it inspire their children to feel the same. Parents also provide the necessary support for their children when difficulties arise because of their faith. With loving support and guidance, children face these difficulties in a stronger and more confident way.

When my older son started first grade, he was very eager to learn new things and to make new friends. As so often happens in life, challenges arrive more quickly than expected. Within the first few weeks of school, his teacher, in a kind attempt to get to know her students, asked how many of them went to church. It seemed that all of the children in the class raised their hands except for him. When he came home that day, he told me what had happened. "Mother, I was the only one," he said. I think it was the first time in his young life that he realized that being a Bahá'í was different from most of his friends.

We talked for a while and the next morning I went to see his teacher. I explained to her that we were members of the Bahá'í Faith and that we did not go to church. I shared with her a picture of the Bahá'í House of Worship in Wilmette, Illinois, so that she could see an example of the Faith. We talked for a few minutes and, later that day, she encouraged my son to show the picture of the House of Worship to his class. This made him very happy because all of the children thought that it was very pretty. At that age, they must have imagined that his "church" was right around the corner and that he must be very lucky to go there.

After this, I made sure that all of my son's teachers were informed about the Faith. I also made sure that their teachers and principals received the list of Bahá'í Holy Days that my sons would be taking off during the year. When the Faith is presented in a pleasant and informative way, people tend to respond positively to it. I never had any problems after that with my son's teachers or their schools. As we teach our children to appreciate the differences in others, let us also encourage them to appreciate the differences in themselves.

Part of identifying with one's faith is developing the courage to stand up for one's beliefs. As children grow older, they will be faced with making decisions about what they believe and about what they will do in certain situations. Developing courage is an important part of this process. It seems that everything of consequence in life takes courage. History is filled with people who took a stand for their beliefs and who found the courage to do so even in the face of danger. We cannot control everything that happens to our children in the outside world. We cannot guard them from unkind words or the attitudes that people take when they are faced with the unfamiliar. But our love, our guidance, and our courage, particularly in times of tests, teach our children that standing up for one's beliefs is possible even in the most difficult of circumstances.

The other factor that greatly influences our children's Bahá'í identities is positive Bahá'í experiences. The richer these experiences, the deeper will be their connections to the Faith. What I found most helpful for my children were experiences that brought them into contact with other Bahá'ís. These experiences not only influenced their attitudes about the Faith, but also made them feel happy about being Bahá'ís. Some of these experiences included: Feasts and Holy Days, Bahá'í children's classes, and Bahá'í Summer and Winter schools. We will discuss these subjects more in depth in the following sections. Through strong and loving parents and through positive Bahá'í experiences, children's identities are strengthened, and they become happier and more confident Bahá'ís.

Feasts and Holy Days

Feasts and Holy Days are special days in the Bahá'í calendar when the community comes together to worship God and to share in fellowship with one another. Feasts are also the times when the Bahá'í community consults together on various aspects of community life. 'Abdu'l-Bahá shares these guidelines for Feasts. He states, *"The believers of God must assemble and associate with each other in the utmost love, joy and fragrance. They must conduct themselves (in these Feasts) with the greatest dignity and consideration, chant divine verses, peruse instructive articles, read the Tablets of 'Abdu'l-Bahá, encourage and inspire each other with love for the whole human race. . . ."*[81]

Children are an important part of Feasts. Their presence brings life and energy to the community. It is important, therefore, for children to be treated lovingly at Feasts. From a letter written on behalf of the Universal House of Justice, we read the following: *"Since children of Bahá'í parents are considered to be Bahá'ís, they are to be encouraged to attend all Feasts, there to share the reading of the Writings and prayers and be bathed in the spirit of the community. It is the hope of the House of Justice that every Feast will be a feast of love when the children will give and receive the tangible affection of the community and its indi-vidual members."* [82] How can we help our children become "bathed in the spirit of the community"? How can we help our Feasts become spiritual "feasts of love"?

There are many ways that we can make our Feasts more meaningful for children. During the spiritual portion, we could involve them in the readings or find innovative ways to help them enjoy the experience of Feast. During the administrative portion, we could plan something special for the children or include them in some of the discussions. During the social portion, we could provide healthy snacks for them to eat and a place for them to play. We could also encourage them to help with refreshments or cleaning up after Feast. Contributing to the Bahá'í Fund, which only Bahá'ís are permitted to do, is a special privilege. A pretty fund box could be provided to make it fun for them to contribute. When children feel loved and appreciated at Feasts, they know that they are an integral part of the Bahá'í community.

Other special days in the Bahá'í calendar are the Intercalary Days or Ayyám-i-Há. These are the four days of the year (five days in a leap year) that are set aside for hospitality, gift-giving, acts of charity, feasting, and rejoicing. My sons always looked forward to Ayyám-i-Há because of the special Bahá'í parties and because of the small gifts that they would receive each day. Ayyám-i-Há is a time of cel-ebration and a time to share our love with family and friends. It is also the time when the adults and youth of the community prepare themselves spiritually for the Fast.

In what ways can we make Ayyám-i-Há special for children? We could decorate the house with flowers or pretty handmade orna-ments. We could plan special parties for the children and invite some of their friends. We could visit the elderly or provide some service for those who are in need. We could invite people over for hospitality and share our homemade treats. Even the simplest of celebrations can be meaningful if love, fun, and fellowship are present.

The most important days of the year are the Bahá'í Holy Days. These are the days when we honor the Báb, Bahá'u'lláh, and 'Abdu'l-Bahá. Some of these days are festive occasions, while others, such as the Martyrdom of the Báb, the Ascension of Bahá'u'lláh, and the Ascension of 'Abdu'l-Bahá are to be observed in a more solemn and reverent manner. Work should be suspended on these days, if possible, and children should be taken out of school.

How can we make the Holy Days more meaningful for children? We could begin by helping them to appreciate the history and sacredness of the day. We could remind them of the importance of good manners and reverence during the Holy Day observance. We could help them prepare themselves physically through the cleanliness and dignity of their dress. Since Holy Day commemorations are sometimes long for younger children, perhaps a children's program could be planned during part of the Holy Day service. During this time, the children could do something interesting and fun, while still in keeping with the dignity of the day. Whatever will make the Holy Days more meaningful for children is important. The spirit of love in the community also contributes to the uniqueness of the day.

Some of the most memorable Bahá'í Holy Days I ever experienced were those I attended in Haifa. What struck me most was the extraordinary sacredness of those days, the supreme dignity that permeated their proceedings, and the overwhelming sense of reverence that moved our very souls. It seemed as if we were experiencing a new standard of worship combined with a new sense of prayer. The diversity of the people also enhanced this experience. They came from all over the world, some dressed in their bright traditional clothes, their faces shining with happiness, and their hearts filled with love. "Alláh-u-Abhá," we would say as we greeted each other in the bright Carmel sun. They resembled beautiful flowers of the garden, all with their own special stories and all with their own special charm. We glimpsed the world as one people and prayed to share this dream with all the world.

The observance of the Ascension of 'Abdu'l-Bahá was especially moving. It began at the foot of Mount Carmel at the old stone house where he lived for the remaining years of his life. That night, as I recall, the air was cool and mild. The moon shone brightly in the darkening sky and the sweet scent of flowers drifted lightly through the air. The hushed whispers of the waiting crowd could be heard as the long line of people inched slowly up the steps. Different kinds of shoes, all shapes and sizes, lay in long rows by the door.

We finally made our way up the steps, passed by the old front door, and entered the front reception hall. We waited there reverently as the long line of people wove their way around the room. And then quietly, ever so quietly, we entered the small bedroom where he had ascended. A soft dim light glowed in the sparsely furnished room. 'Abdu'l-Bahá's worn slippers lay on the floor by the bed. For a few moments, we could pray in this hallowed spot, blessed by the footsteps of our beloved Master. We reflected upon his long years of suffering. We remembered his beautiful smile. A sense of gratitude filled our hearts and a sense of peacefulness surrounded our souls. Then we quietly left the room, placed our shoes upon our feet, walked down the steep, stone steps, and greeted the cool and starry night.

Almost everyone who visits the Bahá'í holy places comes away with this feeling of peacefulness and a growing awareness of reverence that transcends time and space. There are other places where we can experience these feelings as well. I have attended small Bahá'í gatherings where a simple candle, one perfect rose, a picture of 'Abdu'l-Bahá, prayers chanted or spoken, a sweet sense of reverence, and an overwhelming feeling of thankfulness created a spiritual and moving experience for all ages. How meaningful, how beautiful, can we make these sacred days for our children? How sweetly, how reverently, can we honor the Báb, Bahá'u'lláh, and 'Abdu'l-Bahá, our beloved Teachers of the Faith?

Children's Classes

Children's classes are a delightful and inspiring part of the Bahá'í community. Children's classes, which are open to children of all ages, provide young people with the opportunity to study the history and teachings of the Bahá'í Faith, to learn about spiritual concepts and attributes, and to make friends with other children who are learning the same thing. Children's classes also provide that essential combination of learning and fellowship that helps Bahá'í children feel closer to their Faith and enhances their Bahá'í identities.

When my children were young, I knew that they needed something more, in addition to Feasts and Holy Days, to help draw them nearer to their Faith. After studying the Bahá'í writings, I realized that what they needed were regular children's classes. So I decided to set aside one hour a week in the evening for a children's class in my home. I hoped to make it a special time, a time to teach my children about their Faith, and a time to share my love for the Báb, Bahá'u'lláh, and 'Abdu'l-Bahá.

At that time, there were few Bahá'í materials for children and no lesson plans at all. I tried my best to plan meaningful lessons and to make each lesson special by first lighting a candle and saying prayers with my sons. And I always ended each lesson by serving special treats. The classes were simple, sweet, and loving, and consistency was the key. What I found from these simple little lessons was that my sons started looking forward to Bahá'í classes and that their knowledge and feelings about the Faith improved.

Later, a few of us started children's classes in rooms at the local university. We held them every week on Sunday mornings at 10:00 a.m. As our classes grew, our children met other children who shared the same Faith. Many parents came from miles away to bring their children to our school. Eventually, an adult class was started, and soon a fireside class was added. A fireside is an introductory class for those who are interested in learning about the Bahá'í Faith. The school served to unite the Bahá'í communities in a way that had not been possible before. Through the sacrifice and dedication of many parents, Bahá'í classes were held faithfully for many years. Later, children's classes were held in conjunction with devotional gatherings, and both family and friends were invited to attend. I think back with fondness to those classes and I know that my sons do as well. They have shared with me that attending Bahá'í School was one of their most enjoyable experiences as children.

Many years ago, 'Abdu'l-Bahá was asked to give advice on children's classes. He shared these special words,

The Sunday school for the children in which the Tablets and Teachings of Bahá'u'lláh are read, and the Word of God is recited for the children is indeed a blessed thing. Thou must certainly continue this organized activity without cessation, and attach importance to it, so that day by day it may grow and be quickened with the breaths of the Holy Spirit. If this activity is well organized, rest thou assured that it will yield great results. Firmness and steadfastness, however, are necessary, otherwise it will continue for some time, but later be gradually forgotten. Perseverance is an essential condition. In every project firmness and steadfastness will undoubtedly lead to good results; otherwise it will exist for some days, and then be discontinued.[83]

What other subjects should children learn in Bahá'í classes? Bahá'u'lláh states, *"That which is of paramount importance for the children, that which must precede all else, is to teach them the oneness of God and the Laws of God."*[84] To educate children about the oneness of God means to teach them that there is one loving Creator Who has revealed Himself over time through His Manifestations. To educate children about the laws of God means to teach them important spiritual principles, such as loving others, acquiring virtues, and worshiping God. Educating our children about these important principles is a great privilege. So is teaching them about the Báb, Bahá'u'lláh, and 'Abdu'l-Bahá. There are other subjects they could learn as well, depending on their particular ages.

Shoghi Effendi offered his advice on children's classes. He wrote, *"With The Dawn Breakers in your possession you could also arrange interesting stories about the early days of the movement which the children would like to hear. There are also stories about the life of Christ,*

Muḥammad and the other Prophets which if told to the children will break down any religious prejudice they may have learned from older people of little understanding."[85] To educate children about the unity of religion means to teach them that all of the Manifestations of God have come with a specific purpose, one of educating humanity and of helping them to know their Creator. Teaching our children these important principles also helps them to understand people of other faiths and enables them to see the plan of God as it unfolds.

We are fortunate that today many more children's materials are available on these subjects. Bahá'í curriculum guides and other resource materials provide teachers with quick and easy ways to plan special lessons for their students. Teacher training is also increasingly available and helps teachers to feel more competent and prepared.

Another important aspect of children's classes is creativity. Creativity helps students to gain a better understanding of spiritual subjects through innovative means. Puppet shows, arts and crafts, and music or singing make Bahá'í classes more enjoyable and meaningful for children. When the imaginations of children are lovingly nurtured, learning becomes a gift and a joy. End of the year parties, special retreats, or school outings also enhance our children's Bahá'í experiences.

In order to function properly, children's classes must also exhibit certain basic characteristics. What are these characteristics? 'Abdu'l-Bahá writes, *"It followeth that the children's school must be a place of utmost discipline and order. . . ."*[86] Discipline and order allow Bahá'í classes to function more smoothly and help children to learn more easily. When discipline and order are part of the learning environment, children feel more comfortable and safe. Well-planned lessons and orderly classrooms are in the best interests of the child.

Another important characteristic of a Bahá'í school is cleanliness. 'Abdu'l-Bahá states, *"The more cleanly the pupils are, the better; they should be immaculate."*[87] As we have learned, cleanliness influences our spiritual development. The environment in which the classes take place should also be clean and safe. Students should be asked to help clean up after class. Putting away their supplies, straightening their chairs, or sweeping the floor are all opportunities for service. Beauty is another consideration. Could the classrooms be a delight to the eye as well as to the heart?

Children's classes should also be characterized by their courtesy. 'Abdu'l-Bahá states, *"The children must be carefully trained to be most courteous and well-behaved."*[88] Raising one's hand in order to speak, respecting others by good listening, and displaying courtesy and manners are essential behaviors that all children should learn. Children should also show respect for their teachers as well as the home or the building in which classes are being held.

The most important part of any children's class is a kind and loving teacher. Kind and loving teachers share their love for learning and their love for God. Kind and loving teachers understand their students' needs as well as their eager desires to express themselves. It will be the little efforts that they make for their students that will remain with them for the rest of their lives. Every kind word that they speak, every tender touch of their hand, every smile that they show in encouragement, and every compliment that they offer for a job well done help to form a happy spirit in children and teach them what it means to be a Bahá'í.

'Abdu'l-Bahá offers this loving guidance to teachers. He writes, *"O thou spiritual teacher! In thy school, instruct thou God's children in the customs of the Kingdom. Be thou a teacher of love, in a school of unity. Train thou the children of the friends of the Merciful in the rules and ways of His loving-kindness. Tend the young trees of the Abhá Paradise with the welling waters of His grace and peace and joy. Make them to flourish under the downpour of His bounty. Strive with all thy powers that the children may stand out and grow fresh, delicate, and sweet, like the ideal trees in the gardens of Heaven.*"[89]

It is a great honor to be a teacher of young souls. Bahá'u'lláh describes this noble station. He states,

Blessed is that teacher who remaineth faithful to the Covenant of God, and occupieth himself with the education of children. For him hath the Supreme Pen inscribed that reward which is revealed in the Most Holy Book.

Blessed, blessed is he! [90]

Bahá'í Summer and Winter Schools

Bahá'í Summer and Winter Schools, in which all people are welcome to attend, are educational and spiritual retreats that offer parents and children the opportunity to deepen their knowledge of the Bahá'í Faith and to immerse themselves in a Bahá'í experience. Although Summer and Winter Schools are held only once a year, their benefits last a long time. My sons shared with me that some of the happiest moments they ever experienced as children were the times they attended Bahá'í Summer and Winter Schools.

How are these schools organized and what is their purpose? In a letter written on behalf of Shoghi Effendi, we read the following:

He has noted with deepest satisfaction indeed that your meetings have been well attended this year, and that the program had been made as varied and interesting as possible, and combined, as every Bahá'í Summer School should, the threefold features of devotion, study and recreation. Only through such a harmonious combination of these three elements can the institution of the Summer School yield the maximum of beneficent results, and fulfill its true function of deepening the knowledge, stimulating the zeal, and fostering the spirit of fellowship among the believers in every Bahá'í community.[91]

It is precisely this threefold combination of devotion, study, and recreation that makes the Bahá'í schools so successful. The enthusiasm that results from children coming together to share in these wonderful activities is a source of lasting joy. Children enjoy praying together, sharing devotions together, and studying spiritual subjects in a pleasant and supportive environment. They enjoy making new friends and having the opportunity to spend time with them.

I remember with fondness the Bahá'í schools that our family attended in the past. The schools that were held in environments close to nature seemed to be the most memorable. The smell of the woods, the fresh clean air, and the warm glow of bonfires at night under the stars made for exceptional experiences. Singing songs together, sharing meals together, working together, and laughing together for a whole weekend revitalizes our children's spirits and helps them to face the world again when it is time to return to their homes. Permanent Bahá'í schools also offer these same kinds of experiences and have the added advantage of lasting for longer periods of time.

Because Bahá'í schools are so valuable for our children and serve to enhance their Bahá'í identities, we should try our best to help our children attend these schools. Sometimes trusted friends can serve as guardians for older children if parents are unable to attend. Scholarships are sometimes made available for parents or children who are unable to pay for themselves. Even one day at these schools can make a difference in our children's lives. Here they see a much larger picture of the Bahá'í community. Here they find that there are others, beside themselves, who care about the Faith. And here they experience the excitement that comes from learning, praying, and playing together.

What we are doing is making memories for our children—memories of deep spiritual joy, memories of belonging, memories of kindness and love, and memories of complete and conscious happiness. The details, I feel, are less important than the feelings that they come away with afterward. These are the feelings that they will hold in their hearts for years to come. And when times are difficult, as life sometimes is, they can call on those times of joy, those memories they made so long ago in happier times, and they can remember what it means to be a Bahá'í and to be part of this wonderful Faith.

Children's Duty toward Their Parents

As we have learned, parents are entrusted with the sacred duty of loving, of caring for, and of educating their children. In like manner, children are entrusted with the sacred duty of loving, of caring for, and of honoring their parents. Bahá'u'lláh states, *"Say, O My people!*

Show honor to your parents and pay homage to them. This will cause blessings to descend upon you from the clouds of the bounty of your Lord, the Exalted, the Great."[92]

Honoring one's parents has always been a principle of religious belief. The Qur'án encourages children to be kind to their parents. The Bible enjoins children to honor their father and mother. This sacred principle is affirmed, once again, in this new Dispensation. Bahá'u'lláh states, *"The fruits that best befit the tree of human life are trustworthiness and godliness, truthfulness and sincerity; but greater than all, after recognition of the unity of God, praised and glorified be He, is regard for the rights that are due to one's parents. This teaching hath been mentioned in all the Books of God, and reaffirmed by the Most Exalted Pen."*[93]

How should children honor their parents? Children should honor their parents by listening patiently when they speak, by obeying their wishes without arguing, and by treating them with the greatest love and respect. When children honor their parents, they look to them for guidance, they value their opinions, and they trust that they will do their best for them. Children show honor to their parents by appreciating them, by valuing them, and by cherishing them.

Parents who are worthy of this trust treat their children in a gentle and loving manner. They request them to do things in a firm but kind way, and they show consistency in their parenting so that their children know what to expect. Parents who are worthy of this trust show flexibility in certain situations and stand firm in others. Parents should also support each other in their decisions and present a unified front. Because of this, they command their children's respect and create an environment in their home based on mutual consideration and trust.

The honor and respect that is due one's parents should also be extended to one's grandparents, older family members, and other elders in the community. In some cultures, respect for one's elders is still practiced by all members of the community. In these cultures, elders are admired for their wisdom and life experiences. In other cultures, respect for one's elders has been lost and society suffers because of it. Children should learn to love and to respect their elders, especially their parents, because it is essential for the unity of the family and for the welfare of the entire community.

What are other responsibilities of children toward their parents? 'Abdu'l-Bahá states, *"The son . . . must show forth the utmost obedience towards his father, and should conduct himself as a humble and a lowly servant. Day and night he should seek diligently to ensure the comfort and welfare of his loving father and to secure his good-pleasure. He must forgo his own rest and enjoyment, and constantly strive to bring gladness to the hearts of his father and mother, that thereby he may attain the good-pleasure of the Almighty and be graciously aided by the hosts of the unseen."*[94] He also writes, *"Comfort thy mother and endeavor to do what is conducive to the happiness of her heart."*[95]

Honoring one's parents has always been an important part of spiritual growth. By honoring and serving one's parents, children show honor and love toward their Creator, and fulfill a sacred responsibility. Bahá'u'lláh instructs us in this understanding. He states, *"Beware lest ye commit that which would sadden the hearts of your fathers and mothers. Follow ye the path of Truth which indeed is a straight path. Should anyone give you a choice between the opportunity to render a service to Me and a service to them, choose ye to serve them, and let such service be a path leading you to Me."*[96]

The Value of Love, Listening, and Laughter

If we could secretly observe every happy home in the world, what would we discover? What three things would they all have in common? The answer, of course, is love, listening, and laughter. A spiritually happy, healthy home is impossible without these three important elements.

Love, as we have learned, is the primary element. We express our love for our children by spending time with them. When we spend time with our children, we develop a bond of love and trust that is stronger than any influence or any other person. When we spend time with our children, we foresee little problems before they become big ones, and we notice when they are sad or upset even if they do not say a word.

Spending time with our children does not mean merely occupying the same space. It means giving them our undivided attention on a daily basis and helping them to know that they are, along with our spouses, the most important people in our lives. In a difficult world, it is not always easy to spend time with our children. We look, therefore, to 'Abdu'l-Bahá for guidance. He was heard to say, *"Nothing is too much trouble when one loves and there is always time."*[97]

One of the ways that we can spend time with our children is by eating dinner together. This activity, taken for granted in the past, is so often lost in modern society. The sharing of food and fellowship has always been a way of bringing people together. How much more could it be a special time to renew our relationship with our children? Eating dinner together should be a cherished time, a time to enjoy each other's company, a time to share the news of the day, and a time to partake in the simple, nutritious meals that are so necessary for a healthy life. Eating dinner together may not seem that significant, but it is often the simplest things in life that are the most important.

Listening is another way that we express our love for our children. By listening to our children, we offer them a precious gift that no one else can give in quite the same way. What does it mean to be a good listener? We look to 'Abdu'l-Bahá for our example. Howard Colby Ives writes, "I have heard certain people described as 'good listeners,' but never had I imagined such a 'listener' as 'Abdu'l-Bahá. It was more than a sympathetic absorption of what the ear received. It was as though the two individualities became one; as if He so closely identified Himself with the one speaking that a merging of spirits occurred which made a verbal response almost unnecessary, superfluous."[98] Listening with our *hearts* as well as our minds is necessary if we hope to have a close relationship with our children.

How do we find the time to really listen to our children? One simple way is by taking a walk. I recall a young girl strolling down the sidewalk with her mother one Sunday afternoon. It was a beautiful summer's day, and they seemed to be enjoying each other's company. The girl must have been around eleven years old and just on the verge of adolescence. As she happily chattered away, her mother listened patiently. What impressed me most was the ease with which they shared this special time together and the patient desire of the mother to listen to whatever her daughter had to say.

Taking a walk with our children does not cost any money. It does not require special clothes or equipment. It just takes two people who want to spend some time together. If we do not take the time to talk with our children when they are young, they will not take the time to talk with us when they are older.

Spending time with our children may seem routine, even less important at times, but it is precisely these intimate, loving experiences that bond our children to us and protect them from the negative influences that they may encounter in the outside world. An intimate, loving feeling between parent and child cannot be established without sharing these precious moments together and without enjoying all of the wonderful experiences that life has to offer.

Equally important for us, as parents, is to have the courage to say "no" to whatever is not spiritually healthy for our children, whether it is the influence of the media or the influence of others. Our responsibility as parents is not to isolate our children from other people, but to make sure that the *first* influence in their lives is their family and their faith. We accomplish this by following our instincts, by following our hearts, and by following our Faith.

Laughter is another part of this process. Laughter, like love, bonds the hearts together. Laughter was important to 'Abdu'l-Bahá, as was happiness. He was often seen encouraging those he met to be happy and to laugh. *"I want you to be happy . . . ,"* He was heard to say, *"to laugh, smile and rejoice in order that others may be made happy by you."*[99] This was not laughter at the expense of others, but laughter that connects us all in our human experience. Laughing and having fun with our children is one of the most wonderful aspects of being a parent. And laughing and having fun with their parents is one of the most wonderful aspects of being a child. When there is laughter in the home, there is always happiness.

Laughter is important to children. So are gentle, restful times. We should give our children time to slow down, to lie quietly in the warm green grass, to ponder the soft clouds above them, and to gaze at the wonder of God's creation. Children need time to reflect, to imagine, and to dream. Enjoying the soft wind across their faces, the sun warming their arms, and the happiness that comes from experiencing these things with their parents is a great blessing.

When we plant a little seed in the warm, dark earth, we cannot rush it to become a beautiful rose. We must feed it, protect it, and nurture it. We must give it time to grow. Our children are like beautiful roses, shining of face, and filled with all the potential in the world.

'Abdu'l-Bahá encourages us in this endeavor. He writes,

The education and training of children is among the most meritorious acts of humankind and draweth down the grace and favor of the All-Merciful, for education is the indispensable foundation of all human excellence and alloweth man to work his way to the heights of abiding glory. If a child be trained from his infancy, he will, through the loving care of the Holy Gardener, drink in the crystal waters of the spirit and of knowledge, like a young tree amid the rilling brooks. And certainly he will gather to himself the bright rays of the Sun of Truth, and through its light and heat will grow ever fresh and fair in the garden of life.[100]

8

JUNIOR YOUTH: FRUITFUL TREES

*O Lord! I am a child; enable me to grow beneath the shadow
of Thy loving-kindness. I am a tender plant; cause me to be nurtured
through the outpourings of the clouds of Thy bounty. I am a sapling
of the garden of love; make me into a fruitful tree. Thou art the
Mighty and the Powerful, and Thou art the All-Loving,
the All-Knowing, the All-Seeing.*

—*'Abdu'l-Bahá*, Bahá'í Prayers

Time passes quickly, and suddenly our children become junior youth!
How did it happen that they became so smart and grew so tall? Their
incredible energy, their sharp wit, and their great capacity to love all
combine to create such interesting and intelligent individuals, individuals who care deeply about life and who understand more with
the passing of each day. It can be one of the most wonderful ages for
families, and one of the most challenging.

153

Friends and fellowship are very important at this age. Equally important are people who, in addition to their parents, can serve as role models. The years from twelve to fourteen are a critical time in our children's physical and spiritual development and ones that will influence their character for years to come. If offered the proper material and spiritual training, these wonderful souls will become fruitful trees in the garden of life, gifts of love to their parents, and blessings to their community.

Our role as spiritual parents is to be the loving gardeners who nurture these young saplings so that they may grow into tall trees laden with spiritual fruits. As we study the Bahá'í writings, we gain a better understanding of what it means to be spiritual parents and a greater appreciation for our children as spiritual beings. They offer us the guidance that we need in order to continue on our way—renewed, invigorated, and with our sights set firm.

Prayer and Meditation

Prayer and meditation are of vital importance for this age group. The prayers serve to comfort them, to strengthen them, and to help them face the myriad challenges of life. They offer them solace in an ever-changing and often difficult world, and they shower them with guidance and with joy. The Bahá'í family is strengthened through prayer and our young people are empowered by it.

What is prayer? Prayer is communion with God. Bahá'u'lláh states, *"Commune intimately with His Spirit, and be thou of the thankful."*[1] Junior youth who commune with God on a daily basis feel the power of His presence in their lives. This provides them with the spiritual incentive to do what is good and what is true. When junior youth feel a connection to their Creator, they are thankful for this wonderful blessing, and they try to live their lives accordingly. Prayer as a shared and loving experience is an essential part of a spiritual family.

Another way that junior youth can commune with God is through meditation. 'Abdu'l-Bahá states, *"Meditation is the key for opening the doors of mysteries."*[2] What great mysteries lie in our spiritual selves? What great mysteries lie in this creation of God? Meditation is a time to detach ourselves from the material and to focus instead on the spiritual. *"Through the faculty of meditation,"* explains 'Abdu'l-Bahá, *"man attains to eternal life; through it he receives the breath of the Holy Spirit—the bestowal of the Spirit is given in reflection and meditation."*[3]

One of the ways that we can teach our junior youth to meditate is by silently and calmly reflecting on the Word of God. When junior youth reflect upon the Word of God, they are inspired by the beautiful words, they open the *"doors of mysteries,"* and they are connected to their spiritual source. Bahá'u'lláh guides us in this understanding when He states, *"Do thou meditate on that which We have revealed unto thee, that thou mayest discover the purpose of God, thy Lord, and the Lord of all worlds. In these words the mysteries of Divine Wisdom have been treasured."*[4]

We can also teach our junior youth to meditate by "speaking" with their spirit. *"It is an axiomatic fact that while you meditate you are speaking with your own spirit,"* explains 'Abdu'l-Bahá. *"In that state of mind you put certain questions to your spirit and the spirit answers: the light breaks forth and the reality is revealed."*[5] By becoming more attuned to their inner voices and by directing their hearts and minds to God, junior youth receive divine inspiration that will guide them through their daily lives. In a world that is increasingly difficult and seems to have gone astray, it is important for junior youth to find that still, quiet voice within them that leads them to their spiritual selves.

Equally important in the spiritual life of the individual is the role of action. A letter written on behalf of Shoghi Effendi states, *"Prayer and meditation are very important factors in deepening the spiritual life of the individual, but with them must go also action and example, as these are the tangible results of the former. Both are essential."*[6] When we encourage our junior youth to pray and to meditate on a daily basis, when we pray for them every day, and when we remind them of the importance of acquiring virtues, they become better people, people who exhibit such spiritual qualities as truthfulness, kindness, and love. Perhaps 'Abdu'l-Bahá says it best when he states, *"Strive that your actions day by day may be beautiful prayers."*[7]

The Importance of Deepening

As we have learned, study of the Sacred Word is essential to the goal of attaining knowledge. In the Bahá'í Faith, we are encouraged to "deepen" in the writings. What does it mean to "deepen"? A letter written on behalf of Shoghi Effendi states, *"To deepen in the Cause means to read the writings of Bahá'u'lláh and the Master so thoroughly as to be able to give it to others in its pure form."*[8] By carefully reading the writings and by memorizing and reciting the sacred verses, junior youth connect their hearts to the Sacred Word and are able to share it with others *"in its pure form."*

Parents play a unique role in connecting their children's hearts to the Bahá'í writings. By deepening with our children and by sharing with them the spiritual meaning of the words, we help them gain a better understanding of the writings and of the guidance that they offer for our daily lives. Even if we may have difficulties ourselves in understanding the Bahá'í writings, we can still share this precious gift with our children. They may even surprise and delight us, at times, with their keen spiritual perception combined with their pureness of heart.

Junior youth can also deepen in the writings by attending Bahá'í classes, by going to Bahá'í Summer or Winter Schools, by participating in Bahá'í junior youth programs, and by meeting in small groups with their peers. Junior youth especially enjoy working together in groups because they can learn as well as socialize with their friends. Whatever method is used, junior youth learn best if the study sessions are consistent and if they are with people whom they feel comfortable with and enjoy.

Shoghi Effendi encourages young people to study the writings. He states,

> You Bahá'í children and young people have both great privileges and great obligations ahead of you, for your generation will be the ones to help build up a new, better and more beautiful world. . . . You should prepare yourselves for this great task by trying to grasp the true meaning of the teachings and not just merely accepting them as something you are taught. They are like a wonderful new world of thought just beginning to be explored, and when we realize that Bahá'u'lláh has brought teachings and laws for a thousand years to come, we can readily see that each new generation may find some greater meaning in the Writings than the ones gone before did.[9]

Why should we encourage our junior youth to study and to memorize and recite the sacred verses? The answer lies in Bahá'u'lláh's potent words. He states, *"Gather ye together with the utmost joy and fellowship and recite the verses revealed by the merciful Lord. By so doing the doors to true knowledge will be opened to your inner beings, and ye will then feel your souls endowed with steadfastness and your hearts filled with radiant joy."*[10]

Service to Humanity

Service to humanity is an important principle in the Bahá'í Faith. It is also a sacred duty. Our perfect example for a life lived in service to humanity is 'Abdu'l-Bahá. In every aspect of his life, even in his name, "Servant of Bahá," we witness his great desire to serve Bahá'u'lláh, and to serve all of humanity. He writes, *"Think ye at all times of rendering some service to every member of the human race. . . . Be ye sincerely kind, not in appearance only. Let each one of God's loved ones center his attention on this: to be the Lord's mercy to man; to be the Lord's grace. Let him do some good to every person whose path he crosseth, and be of some benefit to him."*[11]

How can we help our junior youth to be of service to humanity? One of the ways that we can do this is by giving them opportunities to volunteer their time. By assisting their parents, grandparents, or other family members as well as helping their friends, acquaintances, or those in need, junior youth learn what it means to be of service. They can also be of service by assisting the Bahá'í community in which they live, such as cleaning the Bahá'í center or volunteering to help with the children.

Another way that we can help our junior youth to serve humanity is by encouraging them to do well in school. By working diligently in their studies and by learning all that they can, they prepare themselves for the future in order to serve humanity through a trade or profession.

Junior youth can further serve humanity by setting good examples for their peers. Through their kindness and character, through their refusal to backbite, through their strength in standing up for their beliefs, and through their dedication to and love for all humanity, they teach others what it means to be spiritual. 'Abdu'l-Bahá instructs us with these words, *"Let him improve the character of each and all, and reorient the minds of men. In this way, the light of divine guidance will shine forth, and the blessings of God will cradle all mankind: for love is light, no matter in what abode it dwelleth; and hate is darkness, no matter where it may make its nest."*[12]

Service to humanity is an important endeavor for young people. By serving humanity, they express their Faith in action, they develop their characters, and they experience the true joy that comes from helping others. Bahá'u'lláh offers these wise words, *"It is incumbent upon every man of insight and understanding to strive to translate that which hath been written into reality and action. . . . That one indeed is a man who, today, dedicateth himself to the service of the entire human race."*[13]

The Value of Friends, Mentors, and the Arts

Friends are important to junior youth. This is the age when the desires and opinions of friends assume a much greater role in their minds than they ever did before. Because of this, we should encourage our junior youth to choose their friends wisely and to choose friends who will have a positive influence in their lives.

Junior youth can make friends at Bahá'í schools, Bahá'í retreats and conferences, and, hopefully, in their own Bahá'í communities.

If there are junior youth in the community, parents can form a junior youth group. A Friday night junior youth group, for example, could consist of prayers, followed by study and creative activities, and ending with refreshments and fellowship. Fun retreats and social outings also bond the junior youth together. What every junior youth needs in order to feel happy about being a Bahá'í is one Bahá'í friend who loves the Faith and who is trying to live a Bahá'í life.

Mentors are also important to junior youth. My sons were fortunate when they were junior youth in that they met two young Bahá'í men who became their mentors. One of them was my son's teacher at Bahá'í Summer School, and the other had just moved into our community. The first, though separated by many miles from my son after Bahá'í Summer School ended, remained his dear friend and is still a friend of his today. The other I befriended when he moved into our community, and he soon became one of the teachers of the Bahá'í youth class.

The reason that these two young men made such an impression on my sons was that they were both in love with the Faith. What junior youth need in order to feel good about being Bahá'ís are people who they can look up to, who they feel that they have something in common with, who are good role models, and who have a love for and dedication to the Faith. They may meet these people only once, but it may be enough to affect them for the rest of their lives. These two young men spent time with my sons only during Bahá'í activities, but they positively influenced the way that they felt about the Faith. I will be thankful in all the worlds of God for these two young men who made such a difference in their lives.

Equally important in the lives of junior youth are the arts. The arts—whether dance, drama, art, or music—bring a spiritual energy to any activity and are particularly effective with junior youth and youth. 'Abdu'l-Bahá spoke highly of the arts. He states, *"All Art is a gift of the Holy Spirit. When this light shines through the mind of a musician, it manifests itself in beautiful harmonies. Again, shining through the mind of a poet, it is seen in fine poetry and poetic prose. When the Light of the Sun of Truth inspires the mind of a painter, he produces marvellous pictures. These gifts are fulfilling their highest purpose, when showing forth the praise of God."*[14]

Whether it is through individual expression or a shared group experience, the arts enhance our lives and enable us to experience this life in a richer and more spiritual way. Junior youth particularly enjoy the arts because they offer them freedom of expression, enable them to show forth praise to God, and fill their hearts with great joy. Let us strive to give our children joyful and artistic experiences, kind and capable mentors, and good and loving friends.

Moderation and Detachment

At no other age, besides that of youth, will the value of moderation and detachment become more apparent. Children should learn these spiritual qualities long before they become junior youth, but they may gain an even greater appreciation for them in light of the experiences they must face as they grow older. Understanding and appreciating moderation and detachment will lead junior youth to a happy and productive life.

Moderation should be practiced in every area of our lives. 'Abdu'l-Bahá writes, *"How often has it happened that an individual who was graced with every attribute of humanity and wore the jewel of true understanding, nevertheless followed after his passions until his excel-*

161

lent qualities passed beyond moderation and he was forced into excess."[15] Moderation protects us from spending our time in less meaningful or less spiritual activities. It also protects us from that which would not be physically or spiritually healthy. Junior youth should be taught to live a life that is in balance and to be spiritually aware of what would not be in their best interests. When they are trained to see the world with spiritual eyes, they recognize what is important in life and what is not.

Moderation should also apply to one's appearance. In the notes to the Kitáb-i-Aqdas, we read the following: "[Bahá'u'lláh] calls upon the believers not to transgress the bounds of propriety and to exercise moderation in all that pertains to dress."[16] Junior youth should be taught to show forth modesty and tastefulness in their dress as well as in their appearance. In doing so, they show respect for others and they show respect for themselves. Bahá'u'lláh calls upon us to observe moderation in all things. It is our duty, as guardians of our children, to enable them to see this spiritual quality reflected in the lives of their parents.

Humanity, likewise, should observe moderation in order to protect the earth and its peoples. Bahá'u'lláh states, *"The civilization, so often vaunted by the learned exponents of arts and sciences, will, if allowed to overleap the bounds of moderation, bring great evil upon men. Thus warneth you He Who is the All-Knowing. If carried to excess, civilization will prove as prolific a source of evil as it had been of goodness when kept within the restraints of moderation."*[17]

Detachment is another spiritual quality that junior youth should learn. Detachment means separating ourselves from that which would not be worthy of our time. Spiritual individuals are aware of the world, but not attached to it. They may want something, but they do not need every new and fascinating thing that comes along. They also understand that this existence is fleeting and that they eventually pass on to the spiritual world. Knowing this, they will not allow anything to come between them and their Creator.

We help our junior youth to understand this spiritual quality by addressing difficult issues on a day to day basis. For example, we explain that the media may identify certain things as important, but this does not necessarily mean that they are. We explain that our culture may hold certain beliefs to be true, but that they may not be true if they are not in keeping with God's laws. We help our junior youth to detach themselves from outside influences by engaging them in meaningful and spiritual activities that are of benefit to them and are of benefit to others. We also help them learn about detachment by exposing them to peoples and cultures that are different from themselves.

Another important aspect of detachment is separating ourselves from those who would not be good for our emotional or spiritual well-being. Detaching themselves from the desires and opinions of friends is difficult for junior youth and youth. Detaching themselves from their friends, especially friends who they have known for a long time, can be even more difficult. We should help our children learn how to be open and understanding of others, while at the same time detaching themselves from those who would prove detrimental to their emotional or spiritual lives.

Whether it is through choice or through ignorance, friends who follow an ungodly path are harmful to our spiritual well-being. Bahá'u'lláh guides us in this understanding when He states, *"O*

Friend! In the garden of thy heart plant naught but the rose of love, and from the nightingale of affection and desire loosen not thy hold. Treasure the companionship of the righteous and eschew all fellowship with the ungodly."[18] Who are the ungodly? Bahá'u'lláh states, *"The company of the ungodly increaseth sorrow, whilst fellowship with the righteous cleanseth the rust from off the heart."*[19]

One of the ways that we can teach our junior youth about detachment is by telling them stories from *The Dawn-Breakers,* a powerful account of the early years of the Faith. In these amazing stories, they learn about the Bábí martyrs who detached themselves from all things, even their lives, in order to serve their Faith. They also discover potent examples in which to compare their own lives when they are undergoing difficulties.

One of the most powerful examples of detachment in the Bahá'í Faith was that of Ṭáhirih, a young woman who lived in Persia during the time of the Báb. Ṭáhirih was a mother, a poet, and a serious student of religion. It is also reported that she was quite beautiful. As a wife in a prominent Muslim family, she seemed to have everything that life could offer. When she learned about the Báb, however, her heart was touched and she knew that she had to accept this new Faith, one that her heart and her mind told her was true.

Ṭáhirih, soon after she declared her faith, began publicly proclaiming the Báb's teachings, a bold endeavor for a woman of that time. She also believed that, in this new dispensation, the status of women would be elevated. Hundreds of people attended her popular and insightful talks, and she won many adherents and admirers of the Faith. Her husband and family tried adamantly to stop her, but she would not be swayed, and the religious clergy became threatened by her powerful influence. Because she refused to give up her Faith and be silent, she was eventually sentenced to death. During the last few hours of her life, Ṭáhirih remained calm, steadfast, and displayed, as one eyewitness has said, a superhuman fortitude. She proclaimed to her captors before her death, "You can kill me as soon as you like, but you cannot stop the emancipation of women."[20] It is through the example of her life and, even more so, in the example of her death that we witness the true meaning of spiritual detachment and we learn how brave one can be when she loves God with all her heart.

Martha Root, a Bahá'í teacher and an amazing example of detachment in her own right, describes this Bahá'í heroine in her book *Ṭáhirih the Pure*. She writes, "O Ṭáhirih! You have not passed away, you have only passed on. Your spiritual, courageous individuality will forever inspire, ennoble, and refine humanity; your songs of the spirit will be treasured in innumerable hearts. You are to this day our thrilling, living Bahá'í teacher. And your work is only beginning, for you will bring our Bahá'í Faith to many millions yet unborn."[21]

We can also teach our children about detachment by telling them stories of the Báb, Bahá'u'lláh, and 'Abdu'l-Bahá. As they become aware of the great hardships suffered by these holy beings in the path of God, they gain a greater appreciation for their Faith and for the sacrifices that it required in order to be born. Detachment may be difficult, at times, to understand. 'Abdu'l-Bahá's words prove helpful. He was heard to say, *"Detachment does not imply lack of means; it is marked by the freedom of the heart."*[22]

As spiritual parents, we need a certain degree of strength, a willingness to go against what others may deem important at the time, and a desire to focus on the spiritual needs of our children. We are also required to be wise custodians of their time and of their boundless energy. Focusing on what will give them true and lasting happiness is our responsibility and this is a spiritual connection to God. Years later, our children may even thank us, as mine did, for not always giving them everything they wanted, but, instead, giving them everything that was truly important.

Tests and Difficulties

Tests and difficulties can occur in any family at any time. It is sometimes when our children become junior youth or youth, however, that these tests and difficulties may become more apparent. Some families find that this age group brings great challenges while others find that it offers some of the happiest moments of their lives.

Tests and difficulties confront our young people from many different sources. One of these is the society in which they live. The messages that they receive from the outside world on a daily basis are often in contrast to the spiritual values that they are taught in the home. It seems that the world is continuing its downward moral spiral even as the forces of good are raising their voices in the world. 'Abdu'l-Bahá warned us of these times when he wrote, *"In a time to come, morals will degenerate to an extreme degree. It is essential that children be reared in the Bahá'í way, that they may find happiness both in this world and the next. If not, they shall be beset by sorrows and troubles, for human happiness is founded upon spiritual behavior."*[23]

Along with the hormonal changes that are occurring within their own bodies, junior youth and youth are confronted with challenges that can only be overcome with the support of strong parents and with a solid foundation of spiritual values. Bahá'u'lláh guides us with these words, *"It is the bounden duty of parents to rear their children to be staunch in faith, the reason being that a child who removeth himself from the religion of God will not act in such a way as to win the good pleasure of his parents and his Lord. For every praiseworthy deed is born out of the light of religion, and lacking this supreme bestowal the child will not turn away from any evil, nor will he draw nigh unto any good."*[24]

As spiritual parents, we must educate our children in the laws of God. These laws, which include the difference between right and wrong, the ways that we should interact with others, and the attitude that we should have toward our Creator, protect and guide us in our daily lives. Young people should also have a clear understanding of their purpose in life. This purpose, as stated in the short obligatory prayer, is to know and to worship God.

Teaching our children to be responsible is another part of spiritual parenting. Learning to take responsibility helps our young people to acquire a sense of pride in their work and encourages them to be more capable human beings. Allowing them to suffer the consequences of their actions also teaches our children that all of their actions have consequences and that they must think before they act and should act in such a way as would honor their Creator. In order for them to learn these valuable lessons, we must set a good example for our children. We must show them generous amounts of love and understanding. And we must show strength.

Children need strong parents. They need parents who will lead them, who will guide them, who will not tolerate disrespect, and who will support and encourage them to be mentally and spiritually strong. When we give our junior youth and youth rules, responsibilities, and boundaries, and make sure that they are enforced, we safe-guard them from making unwise decisions before they are emotion-ally or spiritually mature. As they mature and develop more internal controls and self-confidence, we can give them more freedom, but freedom within limits. And we should always know what they are doing and whom they are with.

Having a close connection with our children at this age is extreme-ly important. Being in touch with their emotional states and helping them to put into perspective what is happening in their lives is our responsibility. We should also foster open and loving communica-tion with our children. Our goal is to raise young people who would rather lead than follow, who would rather say "no" to their friends than disappoint their parents whom they love and respect, and who would rather miss out on something that their friends are doing than act in such a way as would be demeaning to the soul.

Prayers are very important at this time. When we pray with our children, especially at night before they go to sleep, we strengthen their spirits, and we strengthen the parent-child bond. We should also pray *for* our children, especially when they are undergoing dif-ficulties. We are fortunate that 'Abdu'l-Bahá has given us so many beautiful prayers for children. He also offers this tender prayer for children who may require additional help in improving their behav-ior. He writes,

O Peerless Lord! Be Thou a shelter for this poor child and a kind and forgiving Master unto this erring and unhappy soul. O Lord! Though we are but worthless plants, yet we belong to Thy garden of roses. Though saplings without leaves and blossoms, yet we are a part

of Thine orchard. Nurture this plant then through the outpourings of the clouds of Thy tender mercy and quicken and refresh this sapling through the reviving breath of Thy spiritual springtime. Suffer him to become heedful, discerning and noble, and grant that he may attain eternal life and abide in Thy Kingdom for evermore.[25]

This loving and compassionate prayer reminds us that parents make mistakes too and that we are all just trying to find our way in the world. I recall many stories about 'Abdu'l-Bahá and the way that he treated people. It was always with an attitude of love and compassion that he greeted everyone, and when he talked with them he listened patiently and attentively. What he offered each individual was unconditional love and acceptance, the like of which many had never known. He also offered forgiveness, even to his worst enemies. As parents, we should try to be like 'Abdu'l-Bahá and offer our children consistent love, compassion, and patience. Affection also works wonders.

I once met a Bahá'í teacher in the public school system who worked with disadvantaged youth. She had helped them to excel in a particular subject when they did not excel in any other class. "What have you done that is different from everyone else?" I asked her. I was wondering what she could possibly say. "I touch them," she said softly. And then she added, "They are not used to being touched." It was not the answer that I had expected. It was not some theory of education or some particular method of instruction. It was the physical expression of love that made all the difference. A small touch on the hand or a pat on the back gave them the ability to learn, to use their minds, and to explore their capabilities. We must never underestimate what one small, loving gesture can do in the life of a child. What can we do to show our junior youth and youth that they are loved?

The spiritual environment in which our children grow up also has a dramatic influence on their behavior. When something is wrong in the family, it is intimately felt by everyone in the home. Sometimes we find that difficulties with our children are a direct result of difficulties with our spouse. Acting out their need to be recognized within this context of family frustration is often the case for young people at this age. Are there issues that need to be addressed in the family that could improve our children's behavior? Are there issues that need to be addressed that could foster a more loving and spiritual home?

A spouse who does not understand the importance of spiritual parenting is also a great challenge. Sometimes we must be strong and unwavering in our commitment to our children's spiritual education so that our spouses can learn that this is important for children and that it is necessary for their overall development. If we do not spiritually educate our children, who else or what else will fill that void? If we do not fight for our children's right to a spiritual education, who else will give them a spiritual connection to God?

It is also more difficult being a parent when we are undergoing difficulties ourselves. How much more so if one is a single mother, a father of a disabled child, or a grandmother who is raising her grandchildren by herself? At times, it seems that tests and difficulties surround us at every turn. Under these circumstances, we can only rely on the words of Bahá'u'lláh when He states, *"O Son of Man! For everything there is a sign. The sign of love is fortitude under My decree and patience under My trials."* [26]

We must remember that we are never truly alone in our human experience. There are always individuals who are less off than we are. Life is difficult, but there are moments of great beauty. When we build a foundation of prayer and of reliance on God, we discover a source of strength and sustenance that will guide us even in the worst of times. *"Build ye for yourselves such houses as the rain and floods can never destroy,"* counsels Bahá'u'lláh, *"which shall protect you from the changes and chances of this life."*[27] In a turbulent world, the love of God is the only safe haven.

We must share with our children that tests and difficulties are a part of life and that we need them in order to become more spiritual beings. Just as the athlete is given physical challenges in order to reach his physical potential, so are we given spiritual challenges in order to reach our spiritual potential. Tests and difficulties help us to rely upon God and suffering helps us to understand the suffering of others. As we share these spiritual truths with our children, they learn the true meaning of patience, fortitude, and humility. They learn that growing closer to God is the goal and that growing closer to others is what gives us strength.

We may sometimes think that it is difficult to be Bahá'ís and to raise our children as Bahá'ís, but it would be much more difficult to live in this world and not have the guidance found in these writings. The writings give us hope for the future, they offer us glimpses of great beauty, and they provide us with comfort and guidance in times of tests. We must ever strive to be brave and to strengthen the spiritual bonds that unite our hearts with our Creator. We must also strive to raise young people who are mentally and spiritually strong.

When our children have a close connection to their Creator and to His Blessed Beauty, Bahá'u'lláh, they find true happiness, the kind that cannot be shaken by the chances and the changes of this life. 'Abdu'l-Bahá states, *"Man is, in reality, a spiritual being, and only when he lives in the spirit is he truly happy."*[28] By believing in our children, by being aware of their needs, and by giving them a spiritual and a material education, we safeguard their futures and we help them to become happier and healthier human beings.

Nobility

Nobility has nothing to do with kings or queens, with how many possessions we may have, or with what position we may find ourselves in. A person who is blessed with nobility possesses such spiritual qualities as selflessness, honor, virtue, trustworthiness, and character. Bahá'u'lláh states, *"O Son of Spirit! Noble have I created thee, yet thou hast abased thyself. Rise then unto that for which thou wast created."*[29]

All human beings must be spiritually educated in order to rise to the station of their own true selves—the station of spiritual nobility. When children are taught that they are noble beings created by a loving God, they more readily recognize behavior that is demeaning to the soul. They recognize it in art, in music, in others, and in themselves. When they recognize the unique spiritual nature within them and they honor it, they are better able to spiritually direct their lives in the future.

We should train our young people to be strong, to be brave, and to exhibit such spiritual qualities as excellence, refinement, and courtesy. They should be loving examples to the younger children, a support to their parents, and a helper to the elderly. They should also possess a strong sense of honor and dignity. Bahá'u'lláh states, *"Ye are the saplings which the hand of Loving-kindness hath planted in the soil of mercy, and which the showers of bounty have made to flourish. He hath protected you from the mighty winds of misbelief, and the tempestuous gales of impiety, and nurtured you with the hands of His loving providence. Now is the time for you to put forth your leaves, and yield your fruit. The fruits of the tree of man have ever been and are goodly deeds and a praiseworthy character."*[30]

When young people understand that they are noble beings, they know that their lives have meaning and that their purpose is clear. A letter written to young people on behalf of Shoghi Effendi states, *"He hopes that you will develop into Bahá'ís in character as well as in belief. The whole purpose of Bahá'u'lláh is that we should become a new kind of people, people who are upright, kind, intelligent, truthful, and honest and who live according to His great laws laid down for this new epoch in man's development. To call ourselves Bahá'ís is not enough, our inmost being must become ennobled and enlightened through living a Bahá'í life."*[31]

The Value of Love, Communication, and Cooperation

What are the qualities of a spiritual family? Surely, a spiritual family would be one in which love for God, love for each other, and love for humanity would be true and cherished realities. It would also be one in which communication and cooperation would be paramount. As our children grow older, we must find new ways in which to love them, to communicate with them, and to encourage kindness and cooperation in the family.

Love is extremely important to junior youth. Junior youth are very thoughtful, sensitive, and caring individuals who are acutely aware of their environment and of the people to whom they are closest. The loving attention of both parents, therefore, is of vital importance. Their strong presence, their loving concern, and the different ways that they show their children affection all contribute to their children's self-esteem and to their understanding of their place in the world. Fathers, especially, play important roles in the lives of their children at this age. Their firm and loving discipline, their willingness to serve as strong male role models, and their commitment to their children's education all contribute to their children's sense of well-being, direction, and happiness.

When we raise our junior youth in the loving embrace of the family, we protect them from outside influences and we empower them to become strong and independent people. When we show our junior youth love and affection on a daily basis, we fulfill their emotional needs, and we strengthen the spiritual bond that connects us to each other. Laughing and having fun as a family also helps us to appreciate the simple things in life and to put our problems in perspective. When junior youth feel that they are genuinely loved and appreciated by their parents, they know that they are beloved children of God.

Another important quality of a spiritual family is communication. How can we encourage good communication with our children? We can listen to them patiently and lovingly. We can take their feelings and opinions seriously. We can help them to identify the root cause of problems and why things happen the way they do. We can train them to ask themselves, "What would 'Abdu'l-Bahá do in this situation?" And we can try to remember that talking *to* someone is not the same as talking *with* someone, and that lecturing is not the same as guiding our children to do what is right.

Consultation is an additional form of communication. Whereas communication means talking with another person in order to exchange thoughts, feelings, or information, consultation means talking together in order to come to a decision or to find a solution to a problem. *"Take ye counsel together in all matters,"* advises Bahá'u'lláh, *"inasmuch as consultation is the lamp of guidance which leadeth the way, and is the bestower of understanding."*[32] Consulting together as a family helps us to make important decisions, such as planning family outings or deciding how best we can help the environment. It also gives us the opportunity to discuss more serious matters, such as those dealing with the emotional and physical challenges of junior youth.

Another essential quality of a spiritual family is cooperation. Cooperation means that everyone works together for the welfare of the family. This attitude of loving cooperation is not always easily accomplished with our children, but is one that we should try our best to instill. Having patience with each other's shortcomings helps in this endeavor as does encouraging love and kindness through our actions as well as words.

One of the ways that we can encourage cooperation in the family is by working together on family projects. Building a fence together, assisting each other with housework, or hosting devotional gatherings fosters a spirit of cooperation and teaches our children the joy of working together toward a common goal. Equally important is pulling together in times of crisis. The family should be a haven in the storm, a fortress in the mighty winds of change, and a refuge of empathy and compassion.

Parenting is a daily, moment by moment, process. It is making our children, along with our spouses, the first priority in our lives. It is showering them with the warmth of love and affection. It is creating in our home an environment where children feel safe and feel loved. It is educating them in the things of the world and in the things of the spirit. It is giving them to drink of the water of life.

Life is made up of many little moments. And it is these moments, combined together, that make up the fabric of life. If we think of every moment as a sacred gift from God, we know that everything we do has meaning. Every time we tell our junior youth that they are loved and every time we take the time to hug them and to help them is important. Protecting them, leading them, guiding them, and believing in them are our spiritual responsibilities. By believing in their potential to do good, to be amazing human beings, and by seeing them as fruitful trees in the garden of life, we offer our children the vision of who it is possible to become.

This is the meaning of life—to cherish these special moments and to use them in the best way that we can. Our goal is to educate our junior youth to be loving and spiritual human beings, human beings who honor their Creator with every moment of their lives. 'Abdu'l-Bahá encourages us with these words,

As to thy question regarding the education of children: it behooveth thee to nurture them at the breast of the love of God, and urge them onward to the things of the spirit, that they may turn their faces unto God; that their ways may conform to the rules of

good conduct and their character be second to none; that they make their own all the graces and praiseworthy qualities of humankind; acquire a sound knowledge of the various branches of learning, so that from the very beginning of life they may become spiritual beings, dwellers in the Kingdom, enamored of the sweet breaths of holiness, and may receive an education religious, spiritual, and of the Heavenly Realm.[33]

9

YOUTH:
STARS OF THE HEAVEN
OF UNDERSTANDING

O Lord! Make this youth radiant, and confer Thy bounty upon this poor creature. Bestow upon him knowledge, grant him added strength at the break of every morn and guard him within the shelter of Thy protection so that he may be freed from error, may devote himself to the service of Thy Cause, may guide the wayward, lead the hapless, free the captives and awaken the heedless, that all may be blessed with Thy remembrance and praise. Thou art the Mighty and the Powerful.

—*'Abdu'l-Bahá*, Bahá'í Prayers

The years pass by and, before we know it, our children have reached the age of maturity! How quickly, it seems, they have become youth and how proud we are of them! Their sweet, spiritual natures, their incredible enthusiasm for life, and their intense love for humanity all inspire us to become better people and to be even better parents. When our sons reached the age of maturity, my husband and I knew that our full responsibility for their spiritual growth had ended and that it would now rest squarely on their shoulders. We would continue to guide them, to encourage them, and to lovingly support them for the rest of their lives.

The age of maturity is a spiritual milestone in the lives of Bahá'í young people and in the lives of their parents. It is a time when many changes are occurring and many decisions will be made. Confronted with the challenges of this particular age, young people will need to rely upon their faith in God, their strength of character, and their knowledge of the Bahá'í writings in order to determine and to direct their lives. Filled with the love of God, they will meet these challenges with faith and certitude, with courage and detachment, and they will turn to prayer in times of need.

Our role as spiritual parents is to continue to watch over them, to guide them, and to help them in every possible way that we can. If these wonderful youth are given a material and a spiritual education, they will become strong leaders in their schools and communities, shining examples of love and compassion, and brilliant stars in the heaven of understanding. To see our children grow into fine young men and women is a blessing beyond measure.

Obligatory Prayer and Fasting

Spiritual maturity begins when Bahá'í youth reach the age of fifteen. Even though they are still under the guidance and protection of their parents, this is the time when they will make many of the important decisions that will affect the rest of their lives. One of these decisions is choosing whether or not they will continue to live their lives as Bahá'ís. A letter written on behalf of the Universal House of Justice states, *"The importance of attaining spiritual maturity at the age of fifteen is that it marks that point in life at which the believer takes firmly into his own hands the responsibility for his spiritual destiny. At age fifteen, the individual has the privilege of affirming, in his own name, his faith in Bahá'u'lláh. For while the children of Bahá'í parents are considered to be Bahá'ís, they do not automatically inherit the Faith of their parents."*[1]

When young people decide to reaffirm their faith in Bahá'u'lláh, they take on some adult Bahá'í responsibilities. Two of these responsibilities are obligatory prayer and fasting. In the Kitáb-i-Aqdas Bahá'u'lláh states, *"We have commanded you to pray and fast from the beginning of maturity; this is ordained by God, your Lord and the Lord of your forefathers. He hath exempted from this those who are weak from illness or age, as a bounty from His Presence, and He is the Forgiving, the Generous."*[2] Obligatory prayer and fasting are sacred laws, the observance of which are solely between the individual and God.

Bahá'u'lláh offers us three daily obligatory prayers and we are free to choose whichever one that we wish. There are also specific directions that accompany each one. One of these directions is to perform "ablutions" or the washing of one's hands and face as an act of preparation for prayer. Another is turning toward 'Akká and the Shrine of Bahá'u'lláh when we pray. A letter written on behalf of Shoghi Effendi shares the meaning of this simple act. It states, *"This is a physical symbol of an inner reality, just as the plant stretches out to the sunlight—from which it receives life and growth—so we turn our hearts to the Manifestation of God, Bahá'u'lláh, when we pray; and we turn our faces . . . to where His dust lies on this earth as a symbol of the inner act.*"[3] For any other prayer that we choose to say, we can turn in any direction that we wish.

What is the purpose of obligatory prayer and why is it binding? 'Abdu'l-Bahá offers us this loving guidance. He writes, *"O thou daughter of the Kingdom! The Obligatory Prayers are binding inasmuch as they are conducive to humility and submissiveness, to setting one's face towards God and expressing devotion to Him. Through such prayer man holdeth communion with God, seeketh to draw near unto Him, converseth with the true Beloved of his heart, and attaineth spiritual stations.*"[4]

What attitudes, then, should one have while reciting the obligatory prayer? *"While reciting the Obligatory Prayer,"* instructs 'Abdu'l-Bahá, *"one converseth intimately and shareth secrets with the true Beloved. No pleasure is greater than this, if one proceedeth with a detached soul, with tears overflowing, with a trusting heart and an eager spirit. Every joy is earthly save this one, the sweetness of which is divine.*"[5] Humility, devotion, and detachment, therefore, are some of the attitudes that one should have while reciting the obligatory prayer. Another is gratitude. If we look up the word "obligation" in the dictionary, we find that it has several meanings. One of these is "debt of gratitude." We should encourage our young people to think of obligatory prayer as a "debt of gratitude" since, each and every day of their lives, they should thank God for His countless blessings.

Another spiritual obligation of Bahá'í youth at the age of maturity is the recitation of *"Alláh-u-Abhá,"* the Arabic phrase that means "God is Most Glorious." Bahá'u'lláh states, *"It hath been ordained that every believer in God, the Lord of Judgment, shall, each day, having washed his hands and then his face, seat himself and, turning unto*

God, repeat 'Alláh-u-Abhá' ninety-five times. Such was the decree of the Maker of the Heavens when, with majesty and power, He established Himself upon the thrones of His Names."[6] The act of repeating the phrase *"Alláh-u-Abhá"* ninety-five times could be likened to a meditation on the glory of God or to an affirmation of His power and greatness.

Even though the obligatory prayers and the saying of *"Alláh-u-Abhá"* are considered to be individual acts of worship, there are several ways that we could support our youth in the observance of these laws. One of the ways is to encourage an attitude of respect in the family for the time and the quiet that one needs in order to pray and to commune with one's Creator. Another is doing our best as parents to incorporate these sacred laws into our own lives.

Fasting is an additional obligation that Bahá'í young people undertake at the age of maturity. Shoghi Effendi explains the fasting period. He writes, *"The fasting period, which lasts nineteen days . . . involves complete abstention from food and drink from sunrise till sunset. It is essentially a period of meditation and prayer, of spiritual recuperation, during which the believer must strive to make the necessary readjustments in his inner life, and to refresh and reinvigorate the spiritual forces latent in his soul. Its significance and purposes are, therefore, fundamentally spiritual in character."*[7] Fasting is a spiritual endeavor that serves to strengthen, revive, and purify our souls.

There are other reasons given in the writings for the law of fasting. One is to enable us to learn compassion for those who are less fortunate. *"All praise be unto God,"* declares Bahá'u'lláh, *"Who hath revealed the law of obligatory prayer as a reminder to His servants, and enjoined on them the Fast that those possessed of means may become apprised of the woes and sufferings of the destitute."*[8] Learning compassion for others and strengthening ourselves spiritually are two important reasons for fasting. Perhaps the most important reason, however, is simply for the love of God, as Bahá'u'lláh states, *"Observe ye the commandments of God for love of His beauty. . . ."*[9]

How can we assist our young people to have a healthy and meaningful Fast? Some of the things that we could do are to provide them with a good breakfast and a healthy dinner, to encourage them to drink plenty of water before sunrise and after sunset, and to remind them of the importance of proper rest. We could also make the fasting period a special time for the family by eating breakfast together in the morning and by sharing prayers afterward.

Although the Fast can be difficult at times, it can also be spiritually rewarding. Fasting and obligatory prayer are individual, spiritual disciplines that enable us to detach ourselves from the world and to connect our hearts to our Creator. Bahá'u'lláh encourages us in this endeavor. He states, *"Whosoever experienceth the holy ecstasy of worship will refuse to barter such an act or any praise of God for all that existeth in the world. Fasting and obligatory prayer are as two wings to man's life. Blessed be the one who soareth with their aid in the heaven of the love of God, the Lord of all worlds."*[10]

Study of the Sacred Word

Whether youth have been brought up with the Bahá'í writings or are discovering them for the first time, they embark upon a deeper understanding and appreciation for them through study of the Sacred Word. Why should we encourage our young people to study the Sacred Word? The first reason is to know and to love God. 'Abdu'l-

Bahá writes, *"It is the hope of 'Abdu'l-Bahá that those youthful souls in the schoolroom of the deeper knowledge will be tended by one who traineth them to love. May they all, throughout the reaches of the spirit, learn well of the hidden mysteries; so well that in the Kingdom of the All-Glorious, each one of them, even as a nightingale endowed with speech, will cry out the secrets of the Heavenly Realm, and like unto a longing lover pour forth his sore need and utter want of the Beloved."*[11]

When young people take the time to study the Sacred Word, they learn about God's love for them and the importance of their love for God. This love is what carries them throughout their lives and guides them on the straight path. 'Abdu'l-Bahá further educates us in the love of God. He writes, *"This love is not of the body but completely of the soul. And those souls whose inner being is lit by the love of God are even as spreading rays of light, and they shine out like stars of holiness in a pure and crystalline sky. For true love, real love, is the love for God, and this is sanctified beyond the notions and imaginings of men."*[12] What a breathtakingly beautiful vision for our young people—to be as stars of holiness in a pure and crystalline sky!

Another compelling reason for young people to study the Sacred Word is to enable them to follow the commandments of God. Bahá'u'lláh guides us in this understanding. He states, *"The beginning of all things is the knowledge of God, and the end of all things is strict observance of whatsoever hath been sent down from the empyrean of the Divine Will that pervadeth all that is in the heavens and all that is on the earth."*[13] Young people should have a firm understanding that the laws of God are given to them for their protection and for their spiritual welfare. They should also understand that these laws serve to strengthen their spirits and to lead them to do what is right.

Bahá'u'lláh educates us as to the significance of these laws. He states, *"Think not that We have revealed unto you a mere code of laws. Nay, rather, We have unsealed the choice Wine with the fingers of might and power."*[14] It is in their careful study of the Sacred Word that young people learn that it is a privilege to know and to love God and that it is their duty to obey Him. When children are raised with the knowledge and love of God, they respect these spiritual laws as a natural and positive way of life.

How should we encourage our young people to study the Sacred Word? 'Abdu'l-Bahá offers this guidance, *"It is a cause of great happiness to me that you are turning unto the Kingdom of God, that you desire to approach the presence of God and to become informed of the realities and precepts of God. It is my hope that you . . . may investigate and study the Holy Scriptures word by word so that you may attain knowledge of the mysteries hidden therein. Be not satisfied with words, but seek to understand the spiritual meanings hidden in the heart of the words."*[15] Since the sacred words are layered with many meanings, study and meditation are required in order to uncover the treasures that lie hidden within their depths.

Where can young people study the Sacred Word? Young people can study the Sacred Word through individual and family study, through study circles and youth retreats, and through local and regional Bahá'í schools. Young people especially enjoy discussing the Bahá'í writings with their peers. We should try our best, therefore, to give our young people as many opportunities as possible to study with other youth and to discuss the current social and personal issues that the writings so beautifully address. Discussing these issues with their peers is an enlightening and inspiring activity for young people, especially when they are led by an older youth or by a deepened and enthusiastic adult. The unique challenges that young people face at this age can be lightened considerably by simply talking with each other, by supporting each other, and by helping each other understand how the writings can transform lives. When young people take the time to study the writings of Bahá'u'lláh, the Báb, and 'Abdu'l-Bahá, they discover the power and wisdom of the Sacred Word.

The Importance of Reason and Independent Thought

Reason and independent thought are important for people of all ages, but they seem to take on a greater urgency and significance when it comes to youth. The ability to think for one's self and to use one's powers of reason and understanding are crucial for young people as they go through life and face the many challenges that will, no doubt, await them.

'Abdu'l-Bahá shares with us the importance of reason and independent thought when he states,

> God has given man the eye of investigation by which he may see and recognize truth. He has endowed man with ears that he may hear the message of reality and conferred upon him the gift of reason by which he may discover things for himself. This is his endowment and equipment for the investigation of reality. Man is not intended to see through the eyes of another, hear through another's ears nor comprehend with another's brain. Each human creature has individual endowment, power and responsibility in the creative plan of God. Therefore, depend upon your own reason and judgment and adhere to the outcome of your own investigation;

otherwise, you will be utterly submerged in the sea of ignorance and deprived of all the bounties of God.[16]

How does one begin this process of reason and independent thought? 'Abdu'l-Bahá offers this loving guidance. *"Turn to God,"* he states, *"supplicate humbly at His threshold, seeking assistance and confirmation, that God may rend asunder the veils that obscure your vision. Then will your eyes be filled with illumination, face to face you will behold the reality of God and your heart become completely purified from the dross of ignorance, reflecting the glories and bounties of the Kingdom."*[17]

It is our responsibility as parents to encourage our children to reason and to think independently, to use their intuition and common sense, and to trust their inner voices. We should also share our life experiences with our children and remind them to never compromise their principles for any person or any thing. The study of the Sacred Word helps them in this endeavor. Through study of the Sacred Word, they are able to weigh what is told to them by others with what the writings say, and then decide the best course of action to follow. They should also take into account, when making important decisions, the loving guidance and wisdom of their parents.

It follows, then, that young people who are educated in this way will understand that any behavior that is contrary to a spiritual life is not logical and will not offer them happiness nor make their lives better. Filled with the love of God, they will know, without any shadow of a doubt, that it is better to live a life of conscience and to conduct their lives in a manner worthy of their Creator rather than to follow a path that leads to destruction and sorrow. Bahá'u'lláh states, *"They whose sight is keen, whose ears are retentive, whose hearts are enlightened, and whose breasts are dilated, recognize both truth and falsehood, and distinguish the one from the other."*[18]

Religion, as we learn from the Bahá'í writings, must also conform to reason and independent thought. 'Abdu'l-Bahá states, *"Bahá'u'lláh has declared that religion must be in accord with science and reason. If it does not correspond with scientific principles and the processes of reason, it is superstition. For God has endowed us with faculties by which we may comprehend the realities of things, contemplate reality itself. If religion is opposed to reason and science, faith is impossible; and when faith and confidence in the divine religion are not manifest in the heart, there can be no spiritual attainment."*[19] Science and religion, therefore, are complementary, not opposing, forces.

Justice is also linked to the process of reason and independent thought. In the Hidden Words, Bahá'u'lláh states,

O Son of Spirit! The best beloved of all things in My sight is Justice; turn not away therefrom if thou desireth Me, and neglect it not that I may confide in thee. By its aid thou shalt see with thine own eyes and not through the eyes of others, and shalt know of thine own knowledge and not through the knowledge of thy neighbor. Ponder this in thy heart; how it behooveth thee to be. Verily justice is My gift to thee and the sign of My loving-kindness. Set it then before thine eyes.[20]

Justice is important for all people. Without justice, neither governments nor homes can be run properly. Discussing the importance of justice would be a worthwhile activity for young people. "Is this action just?" they could learn to ask themselves. "Does this further the cause of justice for all?" By discussing the moral and spiritual aspects of justice in their lives and in that of society, and by relying on their powers of reason and independent thought, they are better prepared to understand the actions of others and why justice must be present in order for good to prevail.

When young people draw upon their powers of reason and independent thought, when they understand the importance of justice, and when they turn their hearts and minds toward their Creator, they go through life more spiritually aware and spiritually strong. These are the gifts bestowed upon them by their Creator. These are the gifts that enable them to rise to the heaven of understanding!

School and Careers

The pursuit of knowledge is another wonderful gift from God. Bahá'u'lláh states, *"Knowledge is as wings to man's life, and a ladder for his ascent. Its acquisition is incumbent upon everyone."*[21] Young people should strive to acquire knowledge in both their material and spiritual lives. Doing their best in school and working toward their future careers are responsibilities that young people should take very seriously.

The kind of careers that our young people will have in the future largely depends upon their own unique abilities, as well as the persistence and hard work that they put forth to achieve their goals. Although all people are given a certain amount of material and spiritual potential, they can reach that potential only through their own conscious choice and determination. *"Know thou that all men have been created in the nature made by God, the Guardian, the Self-*

Subsisting," declares Bahá'u'lláh. *"Unto each one hath been prescribed a preordained measure, as decreed in God's mighty and guarded Tablets. All that which ye potentially possess can, however, be manifested only as a result of your own volition. Your own acts testify to this truth."*[22]

Volition is defined as the ability to choose, to decide, and to exercise one's own will. It is the responsibility of every individual, therefore, to use his or her volition, to accept the gifts that God has given them, and to rise to their potential. Another part of this process is that of resolve. Resolve is defined as forming a resolution or plan, dedicating one's self to it, and then setting out to accomplish it. Both resolve and volition are necessary for young people as they set out in pursuit of their careers.

What should young people study in school in order to best prepare themselves for the future? Bahá'u'lláh states, *"As to the children: We have directed that in the beginning they should be trained in the observances and laws of religion; and thereafter, in such branches of knowledge as are of benefit, and in commercial pursuits that are distinguished for integrity, and in deeds that will further the victory of God's Cause or will attract some outcome which will draw the believer closer to his Lord."*[23] Integrity, like character, is something that we do not hear about much these days. Integrity is defined as honesty, uprightness, moral virtue, and decency. We understand from the Bahá'í writings that we should strive to be people of integrity. We learn from this passage that the way in which we earn our livings, our livelihood, should also be one of integrity. This understanding helps us to guide our young people toward their futures.

What other things should young people study in school? 'Abdu'l-Bahá writes, *"Let each one who is able and hath a keen desire for it, en-*

roll in higher institutions of learning and study advanced courses in the sciences and arts." [24] Young people who have the desire and ability to go on to higher education should work toward achieving that goal. They should also remember to take the time to develop themselves spiritually.

'Abdu'l-Bahá instructs Bahá'í college students on the spiritual characteristics that they should strive to attain. He states,

> You must become the shining candles of moral precepts and spiritual ideals and be the means of the illumination of others. Clothe your bodies with the robes of virtues. Characterize yourselves with the characteristics of the people of divine morality. . . . Let the corps of professors and the students be impressed with the purity and holiness of your lives so that they may take you as paragons of worthiness, examples of nobility of nature, observers of the moral laws, holding in subordination the lower element by the higher spirit, the conquerors of self and the masters of wholesome, vital forces in all the avenues of life. Strive always to be at the head of your classes through hard study and true merit. Be always in a prayerful state and appreciate the value of everything. [25]

In his loving wisdom, 'Abdu'l-Bahá also takes into account young people for whom higher education may not be chosen or may not be an option. He states, *"Not all, however, will be able to engage in these advanced studies. Therefore, such children must be sent to industrial schools where they can also acquire technical skills, and once the child becometh proficient in such a skill, then let consideration be given to the child's own preferences and inclinations. . . . Let him be placed in that field for which he hath an inclination, a desire and a talent."*[26]

It is our responsibility, as parents, to recognize our children's unique abilities and to guide them on their career paths. We should also remember that work done in the spirit of service is considered an act of worship and that there are many paths to service. *"Hold ye fast unto the cord of material means,"* declares Bahá'u'lláh, *"placing your whole trust in God, the Provider of all means. When anyone occupieth himself in a craft or trade, such occupation itself is regarded in the estimation of God as an act of worship; and this is naught but a token of His infinite and all-pervasive bounty."*[27]

Whatever young people choose to do in their lives, they should do it to the best of their abilities. A letter to Bahá'í youth from the Universal House of Justice offers these inspiring words,

> *Rejecting the low sights of mediocrity, let them scale the ascending heights of excellence in all they aspire to do. May they resolve to elevate the very atmosphere in which they move, whether it be in the school rooms or halls of higher learning, in their work, their recreation, their Bahá'í activity or social service.*
>
> *Indeed, let them welcome with confidence the challenges awaiting them. Imbued with this excellence and a corresponding humility, with tenacity and a loving servitude, today's youth must move towards the front ranks of the professions, trades, arts and crafts which are necessary to the further progress of humankind—this to ensure that the spirit of the Cause will cast its illumination on all these important areas of human endeavour.*[28]

193

The attainment of knowledge should not end with one's school career. Instead, it should be a lifelong goal for every human being. 'Abdu'l-Bahá offers us this loving counsel,

> The attainment of the most great guidance is dependent upon knowledge and wisdom, and on being informed as to the mysteries of the Holy Words. Wherefore must the loved ones of God, be they young or old, be they men or women, each one according to his capabilities, strive to acquire the various branches of knowledge, and to increase his understanding of the mysteries of the Holy Books. . . .
>
> . . . Let the loved ones of God . . . bestir themselves and spare no efforts to acquire the various current branches of knowledge, both spiritual and secular, and of the arts.[29]

Bahá'í Youth Retreats and Conferences

Bahá'í youth retreats and conferences are some of the most wonderful activities that young people can attend because they generate an energy and excitement that few other Bahá'í activities can surpass. Whether it is a weekend retreat at someone's home in their own community or a large Bahá'í conference in another state, young people enjoy making friends and experiencing the joy and fellowship that characterize Bahá'í youth gatherings.

It should not be a surprise to parents that young people need each other and that they need to be together in a loving and supportive environment. Bahá'í youth retreats and conferences provide this loving and supportive environment, one that is far removed from the dictates and pressures of modern life. There is also a strength in numbers that no one can deny. This is particularly true for Bahá'í youth who rarely get the chance to go to school with other Bahá'ís or to interact with many Bahá'ís their own age unless they live in a large Bahá'í community. Bahá'í youth retreats and conferences give them this sense of community, one where they are completely accepted for who they are and where they can feel perfectly free to express themselves spiritually. This acceptance strengthens their commitment to their Faith and enhances their Bahá'í identities.

It is not enough to wait for our Local Spiritual Assemblies or for other Bahá'í committees to plan special activities for our youth. As parents, we must evaluate their particular needs and then make plans accordingly. Social interaction with Bahá'ís is imperative in this day when all around them can be found messages that are in complete conflict with the Faith. Close bonds of friendship and peer pressure of the positive kind are essential if we are to spiritually support our youth during these very critical years. The love and friendship that they experience with their Bahá'í peers does more than any lecture from their parents ever could. They come away from these Bahá'í activities renewed, revitalized, and with a desire to live a more spiritual life.

The ability to spend time together, to strengthen the bonds of love and friendship, and to make lifelong friends not only make our youth happier, they make the Faith more meaningful. By deepening together, by praying together, by talking together, and by having fun together, young people learn that the Faith can touch lives and guide them on the straight path. There is nothing more powerful than to be in a room filled with Bahá'í youth who are praying and who are set ablaze with the love of God. How wonderful to be a Bahá'í youth in this day!

The Year of Service

Bahá'í youth are encouraged, while they are still young and before they have taken on the responsibilities of marriage and family, to give some of their time in service to their Faith. This period of service can last for a few weeks, for a few months, or even for a whole year. Bahá'u'lláh states, *"Blessed is he who in the prime of his youth and the heyday of his life will arise to serve the Cause of the Lord of the beginning and of the end, and adorn his heart with His love. The manifestation of such a grace is greater than the creation of the heavens and of the earth. Blessed are the steadfast and well is it with those who are firm."*[30]

There are many ways in which Bahá'í youth can be of service to their Faith and also be of service to humanity. One of the ways is to serve the Bahá'í community in which they live. Teaching children's classes, mentoring junior youth, planning devotional meetings, or assisting with Bahá'í Holy Days are some of the ways that Bahá'í youth can be of service. They can also be of service by visiting the sick or elderly in their community.

Another avenue of service for Bahá'í youth is volunteering their time at the permanent Bahá'í schools in their own country. These unique experiences give young people an opportunity to meet other Bahá'í youth, to live and work in a Bahá'í environment, and to use their energy and enthusiasm to do work that is greatly needed, such as helping in the kitchen or assisting with children's classes. There are many opportunities for short-term or long-term periods of service and these can be found by contacting one's National Spiritual Assembly.

Other opportunities for service come from volunteering in Bahá'í service projects throughout the world. Our oldest son traveled to Honduras when he was only seventeen years old. He went for a monthlong period of service at a small Bahá'í hospital. He dug trenches, traveled by foot for miles in pristine jungles, slept in hammocks, and rode in handmade canoes to educate families about AIDS and to share with them the message of Bahá'u'lláh. He met many beautiful children who had few material possessions, but who possessed a great wealth of happiness and enthusiasm. He came back physically stronger, speaking Spanish, and with a better understanding that happiness is not primarily dependent on material wealth. He also came back with a new appreciation for his Faith and with a greater respect for those who serve it in this way.

Our younger son, at the age of twenty-one, served for one year at the Bahá'í World Center in Haifa. He worked as a security guard in the beautiful Bahá'í gardens. Although his job was difficult at times, he felt extremely blessed to be in the Bahá'í gardens and to meet the many visitors who came from far away to see them. He also appreciated his time spent in prayer at the Shrines and making friends with other Bahá'í youth who served there from all over the world.

A few years earlier, our family was living in Jerusalem because my husband was the Jerusalem Representative from the Bahá'í International Community. It was during this time that my youngest son had the opportunity to go on a teaching trip to Kenya and Uganda with a group of Bahá'í youth. He was excited to go, but he had no idea how much he would fall in love with the people, the land, and the spirit that he felt radiating everywhere. He left his heart in Africa and still hopes to return one day.

When young people have the opportunity to serve others and to experience different peoples and cultures, they acquire a new understanding and appreciation that affects them for the rest of their lives. Although some service opportunities may prove difficult, there are still important lessons to be learned by youth who choose to serve their Faith in this way. Through these humble acts of service, they become more responsible and caring people, they learn that life has greater meaning and purpose than their popular culture may suggest, and they experience the true bounty of loving and serving others. 'Abdu'l-Bahá shares with us these inspiring words. He states, *"Therefore, order your lives in accordance with the first principle of the divine teaching, which is love. Service to humanity is service to God. Let the love and light of the Kingdom radiate through you until all who look upon you shall be illumined by its reflection. Be as stars, brilliant and sparkling in the loftiness of their heavenly station."*[31]

Teaching

Sharing the message of Bahá'u'lláh has always been an important role for Bahá'í youth, both in the past and in the present. A letter from the Universal House of Justice explains the role that youth have played in the history of the Faith. It states,

> *From the very beginning of the Bahá'í Era, youth have played a vital part in the promulgation of God's Revelation. The Báb Himself was but twenty-five years old when He declared His Mission, while many of the Letters of the Living were even younger. The*

Master, as a very young man, was called upon to shoulder heavy responsibilities in the service of His Father . . . and His brother, the Purest Branch, yielded up his life to God in the Most Great Prison at the age of twenty-two. . . . Shoghi Effendi was a student at Oxford when called to the throne of his guardianship, and many of the Knights of Bahá'u'lláh . . . were young people. Let it, therefore, never be imagined that youth must await their years of maturity before they can render invaluable services to the Cause of God.[32]

In order to share their Faith wisely, young people should first study the words of Bahá'u'lláh when He states,

O Son of Dust! The wise are they that speak not unless they obtain a hearing, even as the cup-bearer, who proffereth not his cup till he findeth a seeker, and the lover who crieth not out from the depths of his heart until he gazeth upon the beauty of his beloved. Wherefore sow the seeds of wisdom and knowledge in the pure soil of the heart, and keep them hidden, till the hyacinths of divine wisdom spring from the heart and not from mire and clay.[33]

Sharing the message of Bahá'u'lláh should always be done with a pure heart, with a radiant spirit, and with wisdom and courtesy.

Young people are also advised to share their Faith by showing sincere love and benevolence toward others. *"Show forbearance and benevolence and love to one another,"* counsels Bahá'u'lláh. *"Should anyone among you be incapable of grasping a certain truth, or be striving to comprehend it, show forth, when conversing with him, a spirit of extreme kindliness and goodwill."*[34]

Last, but not least, young people are advised to share their Faith by being good examples for their peers. A letter written on behalf of Shoghi Effendi encourages Bahá'í youth in this endeavor. It states, *"For the Bahá'í youth constitute the main active element in the Cause. Theirs is the duty not only to study and to spread the Teachings but to put them into actual practice. It is hoped that you will increasingly mirror forth the beauty and the power of the principles of the Faith and will become shining examples to every Bahá'í whose sole aim in life is to scale the heights which Bahá'u'lláh has summoned His followers to attain."*[35]

In what ways can young people find opportunities in which to share their Faith? One of the ways is by participating in Bahá'í college clubs on campus. Our own two sons were members of a Bahá'í college club whose primary purpose was to promote the oneness of humanity. One week the club would offer a discussion on the Bahá'í Faith and the next week a regular club meeting would be held. The Bahá'í Club also planned coffee houses, picnics, and recreational activities so that all of their members could enjoy fellowship with one another. The members, both Bahá'í and non-Bahá'í, formed close bonds of friendship during this time, and, years later, they still remember it as a very happy time in their lives.

There have been many great teachers in the Bahá'í Faith, but one individual stands out from all the rest. At a time when it was unusual for a woman to have a career or to travel by herself, this remarkable individual traveled around the world more than once, with little money and under often dangerous conditions, to share the message that she loved so well. Who was this individual? This amazing individual was Martha Root.

Martha Root was born in the United States in 1872. When she grew up, she became a writer who made her living by writing newspaper articles. In 1908 she was introduced to the Bahá'í Faith, and a year later became a Bahá'í at the age of thirty-seven. When 'Abdu'l-Bahá came to America in 1912, she was fortunate enough to attain his presence and soon afterward proposed an extensive teaching trip around the world. This was the beginning of many teaching trips that she would take on behalf of the Bahá'í Faith.

One example of her extraordinary ability to teach was her meeting with Queen Marie of Romania. From the inspiring book *Martha Root: Lioness at the Threshold,* we read the following: "Martha, who believed that even a queen should have the message of Bahá'u'lláh, had been told that it was impossible to see Her Majesty, that she was in a period of personal sorrow and was receiving no one."[36] Unperturbed, Martha sent her a picture of 'Abdu'l-Bahá, along with Dr. Esselmont's book, *Bahá'u'lláh and the New Era.* It turns out that the queen stayed up until 3:00 a.m. that night reading the book, and, the next day, sent an invitation for Martha to meet her.

The queen must have been quite moved by Martha and by the Bahá'í Faith because, five months later, she wrote this heartfelt and sincere letter that was published in the Toronto Daily Star. It read,

A WOMAN brought me the other day a Book. I spell it with a capital letter because it is a glorious Book of love and goodness, strength and beauty.

She gave it to me because she had learned I was in grief and sadness and wanted to help. . . . She put it into my hands saying: "You seem to live up to His teachings." And when I opened the Book I saw it was the word of 'Abdu'l-Bahá, prophet of love and kindness, and of his father the great teacher of international good-will and understanding—of a religion which links all creeds.

Their writings are a great cry toward peace, reaching beyond all limits of frontiers, above all dissension about rites and dogmas. It is a religion based upon the inner spirit of God, upon that great, not-to-be-overcome verity that God is love, meaning just that. It teaches that all hatreds, intrigues, suspicions, evil words, all aggressive patriotism even, are outside the one essential law of God, and that special beliefs are but surface things whereas the heart that beats with divine love knows no tribe nor race.

It is a wondrous Message that Bahá'u'lláh and his son 'Abdu'l-Bahá have given us. They have not set it up aggressively knowing that the germ of eternal truth which lies at its core cannot but take root and spread.

There is only one great verity in it: Love, the mainspring of every energy, tolerance towards each other, desire of understanding each other, knowing each other, helping each other, forgiving each other.

It is Christ's Message taken up anew, in the same words almost, but adapted to the thousand years and more difference that lies between the year one and today. No man could fail to be better because of this Book.

I commend it to you all. If ever the name Bahá'u'lláh or 'Abdu'l-Bahá comes to your attention, do not put their writings from you. Search out their Books, and let their glorious, peace-bringing, love-creating words and lessons sink into your hearts as they have into mine

One's busy day may seem too full for religion. Or one may have a religion that satisfies. But the teachings of these gentle, wise and kindly men are compatible with all religion, and with no religion.

Seek them, and be the happier.[37]

After this wonderful meeting with Queen Marie, Martha went on to teach for many more years in places as far away as Japan, India, and China, even though she was suffering from breast cancer. She traveled far and wide because of her great love for Bahá'u'lláh and for His son, 'Abdu'l-Bahá. Marzieh Gail, a well-known Bahá'í, wrote, "And so on and on she traveled—not young or strong, not beautiful, not rich, alone, and more than once in terrible danger—on and on, for twenty years. . . . [S]he carried on with her work until, far from home, she stumbled and fell 'in her tracks.'"[38] Like a bright morning star, Martha Root taught the message of Bahá'u'lláh in the earliest days of our Faith.

During the last few days of her life, Martha wrote one final letter to family and friends. In it, she shared these poignant words. She wrote,

I am so near the shores of Eternity. . . .

I thank you each and every one for all that you will do to help me, and I thank you for your love. I do not speak, so late tonight, of the glorious side of life after death. We shall all walk together arm in arm you and I, and in the mystery of God the Bahá'ís will confere [sic] together, understand each other, and I say to you, beloved of my heart, I am glad to go through this terrible agony, for if it came it must have come for a purpose to each one of us. If our love for each other has been deepened, if this servant has been able to witness for her Lord . . . then I have not come in vain. Everything has been successful.[39]

Because of her vast teaching travels across the globe, Shoghi Effendi conferred upon Martha Root the title of "Hand of the Cause of God" after her death in 1939. He also offered this fitting tribute. *"To Martha Root,"* he wrote, *"that archetype of Bahá'í itinerant teachers and the foremost Hand raised by Bahá'u'lláh since 'Abdu'l-Bahá's passing, must be awarded, if her manifold services and the supreme act of her life are to be correctly appraised, the title of Leading Ambassadress of His Faith and Pride of Bahá'í teachers, whether men or women, in both the East and the West."*[40]

We gain much inspiration from individuals like Martha Root, who gave their time and sacrificed their lives so that humanity could learn of these beautiful teachings. May our own dear youth gain inspiration from these stories and share this loving message with every soul who yearns for truth. Bahá'u'lláh encourages them with these words, *"Assist ye, O My people, My chosen servants who have arisen to make mention of Me among My creatures and to exalt My Word throughout My realm. These, truly, are the stars of the heaven of My loving providence and the lamps of My guidance unto all mankind."*[41]

Distinction

Distinction is an important attribute that young people should strive to attain. 'Abdu'l-Bahá tells us, *"I desire distinction for you."*[42]

What kind of distinction does he refer to in this passage? He answers with these kind words,

For you I desire spiritual distinction—that is, you must become eminent and distinguished in morals. In the love of God you must become distinguished from all else. You must become distinguished for loving humanity, for unity and accord, for love and justice. In brief, you must become distinguished in all the virtues of the human world—for faithfulness and sincerity, for justice and fidelity, for firmness and steadfastness, for philanthropic deeds and service to the human world, for love toward every human being, for unity and accord with all people, for removing prejudices and promoting international peace. Finally, you must become distinguished for heavenly illumination and for acquiring the bestowals of God.[43]

Young people who understand the importance of spiritual distinction know that being different from others is a good thing if it is for the right reasons. Some of these reasons should include making good choices, getting good grades, being self-disciplined, and conducting oneself in a dignified manner. Other reasons should include abstaining from drugs, alcohol, and smoking, possessing moral courage, and loving and serving God. A letter written on behalf of Shoghi Effendi states, *"To deepen their knowledge, to perfect themselves in the Baháʼí standards of virtue and upright conduct, should be the paramount duty of every young Baháʼí."*[44]

Baháʼuʼlláh also tells us that individuals should be distinguished by their deeds. He states, *"Guidance hath ever been given by words, and now it is given by deeds. Everyone must show forth deeds that are pure and holy, for words are the property of all alike, whereas such deeds as these belong only to Our loved ones. Strive then with heart and soul to distinguish yourselves by your deeds. In this wise We counsel you in this holy and resplendent tablet."*[45]

In order for young people to understand the high level of distinction to which they should aspire, they must first study the words of Bahá'u'lláh when He states, *"How resplendent the luminaries of knowledge that shine in an atom, and how vast the oceans of wisdom that surge within a drop! To a supreme degree is this true of man, who, among all created things, hath been invested with the robe of such gifts, and hath been singled out for the glory of such distinction. For in him are potentially revealed all the attributes and names of God to a degree that no other created being hath excelled or surpassed."*[46] How beautiful are the words of Bahá'u'lláh! And how well they express our great spiritual potential!

The Bahá'í writings offer us not only the knowledge of how we should live, but also the knowledge of who we can become. By sharing these precious words with our children, we give them the knowledge of who they are as spiritual beings as well as the vision of who they can become. Through the study of Bahá'u'lláh's words, they are educated as to their spiritual potential and to the spiritual potential to which we all have been endowed. Bahá'u'lláh states, *"O friends! Be not careless of the virtues with which ye have been endowed, neither be neglectful of your high destiny. . . . Ye are the stars of the heaven of understanding, the breeze that stirreth at the break of day, the soft-flowing waters upon which must depend the very life of all men. . . ."*[47]

Looking toward Marriage

Marriage in the Bahá'í Faith is a sacred bond, a close friendship, and a strong commitment between two people who love each other and who promise to abide by the will of God. As parents, we pray that our children will find that "special someone" who will love them and care for them even as we have loved and cared for them from the moment they were born. Our own good examples as well as our positive attitudes about marriage influence our young people as they look toward marriage and begin their search for that special person.

How do we encourage our young people to look for the right person? First of all, we must tell them that they should look at a person's character. *"Bahá'í marriage,"* 'Abdu'l-Bahá explains, *"is the commitment of the two parties one to the other, and their mutual attachment of mind and heart. Each must, however, exercise the utmost care to become thoroughly acquainted with the character of the other, that the binding covenant between them may be a tie that will endure forever."*[48]

Although physical attraction between a man and a woman is important, it should not be the only criteria on which to base a lifetime of commitment. It is the character of a person that matters most, especially as the years go by. We should share with our children that learning about another person's character takes time and effort, that it will help them to know who the person truly is, and that there is a difference between real love and physical attraction. These words of wisdom are best shared with our young people, not in lectures, but in quiet, loving moments.

'Abdu'l-Bahá instructs us as to the physical and spiritual aspects of Bahá'í marriage. He writes,

Marriage, among the mass of the people, is a physical bond, and this union can only be temporary, since it is foredoomed to a physical separation at the close.

Among the people of Bahá, however, marriage must be a union of the body and of the spirit as well, for here both husband and wife are aglow with the same wine, both are enamored of the same matchless Face, both live and move through the same spirit, both are illumined by the same glory. This connection between them is a spiritual one, hence it is a bond that will abide forever. Likewise do they enjoy strong and lasting ties in the physical world as well, for if the marriage is based both on the spirit and the body, that union is a true one, hence it will endure. . . .

When, therefore, the people of Bahá undertake to marry, the union must be a true relationship, a spiritual coming together as well as a physical one, so that throughout every phase of life, and in all the worlds of God, their union will endure; for this real oneness is a gleaming out of the love of God." [49]

Another consideration for Bahá'í marriage is that of chastity. Chastity, as defined in the Bahá'í writings, is a purity of the body as well as a purity of the spirit. Young people should be encouraged to practice chastity before marriage because it protects them from experiencing emotional, spiritual, and physical difficulties. A letter written on behalf of the Universal House of Justice states, *"As to chastity, this is one of the most challenging concepts to get across in this very permissive age, but Bahá'ís must make the utmost effort to uphold Bahá'í standards, no matter how difficult they may seem at first. Such efforts will be made easier if the youth will understand that the laws and standards of the Faith are meant to free them from untold spiritual and moral difficulties in the same way that a proper appreciation of the laws of nature enables one to live in harmony with the forces of the planet.*"[50]

Young people should also be encouraged to practice chastity because it contributes to the happiness and well-being of their future marriages. A letter written on behalf of the Universal House of Justice states, *"It is the sacred duty of parents to instill in their children the exalted Bahá'í standard of moral conduct, and the importance of adherence to this standard cannot be over-emphasized as a basis for true happiness and for successful marriage."*[51]

The topic of chastity seems best addressed if done in a group setting with youth (or junior youth) who have gathered for this very purpose. Deepening on the spiritual importance of chastity as well as deepening on other relevant topics enables our young people to become spiritually informed and to feel emotionally supported by their peers. Through study of the Bahá'í writings and through frank and loving consultation, young people learn that chastity is a noble and worthy goal.

An additional consideration for Bahá'í marriage is looking for someone who will be a good parent. A strong and loving mother and father are necessary if their children are to be strong and loving individuals. Choosing the right spouse makes a difference in the character of our children. Someone who cares about children, who is kind and loving toward them, and who is concerned about their welfare will make a better parent than someone who does not possess these qualities. We are also reminded of the importance of the mother's role. 'Abdu'l-Bahá states, *"If the mother is educated then her children will be well taught. When the mother is wise, then will the children be led into the path of wisdom. If the mother be religious she will show her children how they should love God. If the mother is moral she guides her little ones into the ways of uprightness."*[52] He also states, *"If, as she ought, the mother possesseth the learning and accomplishments of humankind, her children, like unto angels, will be fostered in all excellence, in right conduct and beauty."*[53]

Our last major responsibility as Bahá'í parents is to give our children permission to get married. When Bahá'í couples wish to get married, they must first ask their parents for consent. 'Abdu'l-Bahá writes, *"As for the question regarding marriage under the Law of God: first thou must choose one who is pleasing to thee, and then the matter is subject to the consent of father and mother. Before thou makest thy choice, they have no right to interfere."*[54] 'Abdu'l-Bahá emphasizes, in this statement, that Bahá'í marriages are not "arranged" by one's parents or by other people, but that the individuals are free to choose whom they wish.

What, then, is the Bahá'í law concerning consent and what is the reason for this law? Bahá'u'lláh states, *"It hath been laid down in the Bayán that marriage is dependent upon the consent of both parties. Desiring to establish love, unity and harmony amidst Our servants, We have conditioned it, once the couple's wish is known, upon the permission of their parents, lest enmity and rancor should arise amongst them. And in this We have yet other purposes. Thus hath Our commandment been ordained."*[55] Shoghi Effendi further explains the reason for this law. He writes, *"This great law He has laid down to strengthen the social fabric, to knit closer the ties of the home, to place a certain gratitude and respect in the hearts of children for those who have given them life and sent their souls out on the eternal journey towards their Creator."*[56]

What is the responsibility of parents regarding consent and what is the responsibility of children toward their parents? A letter from the Universal House of Justice states,

> *It is perfectly true that Bahá'u'lláh's statement that the consent of all living parents is required for marriage places a grave responsibility on each parent. When the parents are Bahá'ís they should, of course, act objectively in withholding or granting their approval. They cannot evade this responsibility by merely acquiescing in their child's wish, nor should they be swayed by prejudice; but, whether they be Bahá'í or non-Bahá'í, the parents' decision is binding, whatever the reason that may have motivated it. Children must recognize and understand that this act of consenting is the duty of a parent. They must have respect in their hearts for those who have given them life, and whose good pleasure they must at all times strive to win.*[57]

Giving our children permission to get married is a weighty responsibility and one that we must take very seriously. It is also a matter of trust. We can never really know if our children will have a happy marriage. We can only make, through prayerful consideration and by taking into account the readiness and maturity of the two individuals, the best decision that we can. If our children have proven themselves to have made good decisions in the past and if they have been raised to understand the spiritual implications of marriage, we must trust them to make the right decision in this case, a decision that is based on true love and real commitment.

'Abdu'l-Bahá enlightens Bahá'í couples on the spiritual significance of marriage. He writes,

O ye two believers in God! The Lord, peerless is He, hath made woman and man to abide with each other in the closest companionship, and to be even as a single soul. They are two helpmates, two intimate friends, who should be concerned about the welfare of each other.

If they live thus, they will pass through this world with perfect contentment, bliss, and peace of heart, and become the object of divine grace and favor in the Kingdom of heaven. . . .

Strive, then, to abide, heart and soul, with each other as two doves in the nest, for this is to be blessed in both worlds.[58]

The Value of Love, Respect, and Trust

A good relationship between parents and youth is dependent upon three important qualities, those of love, respect, and trust. Love is by far the most important quality. We express our love for our young people in many different ways. One of the ways is to show them affection. A soft and loving touch or kind and loving words show our youth how much we care for them. Warm hugs and sweet kisses at the appropriate time and place are also necessary. Expressing our love for our young people in these ways is far more important than anything else that we could ever do for them. And wise parents know that material things can never be good substitutes for unconditional love.

We also express our love for our young people by spending time with them. Spending time together as a family is one of life's greatest pleasures. Doing simple things together, such as riding bikes, taking walks, or sharing common interests or hobbies give us a chance to communicate with our children and give them a chance to communicate with us. By spending time with our youth in a loving and attentive manner, we give them the opportunity to open up to us if there is something that they wish to share. Our goal is to spend enough time with our youth that communicating with their parents is just a natural part of life.

Another important quality of a good relationship is that of respect. Respect means that we should take into account the rights and needs of every member of the family. 'Abdu'l-Bahá tells us that each member of the family has certain basic rights as individuals as well as certain obligations to each other. He states, *"Just as the son has certain obligations to his father, the father, likewise, has certain obligations to his son. The mother, the sister and other members of the household have their certain prerogatives. All these rights and prerogatives must be conserved, yet the unity of the family must be sustained. The injury of one shall be considered the injury of all; the comfort of each, the comfort of all; the honor of one, the honor of all."*[59] Respecting each other as individuals is essential for the unity of the family.

Having a good relationship with others also means having respect for oneself. We should teach our young people that they should have respect for themselves because they are created in the image of God and are His precious children. Some of the ways that they show respect for themselves are by taking care of their bodies and by using them to do God's Will, by taking care of their minds and by using them to the best of their abilities, and by honoring their Creator by living as praiseworthy and noble beings.

Trust is another quality of a good relationship. We gain our children's trust by being consistent in our parenting, by helping them to understand our expectations fully, and by communicating our wishes for them in a loving and responsible manner. We also gain our children's trust by being available when they need us, by showing real concern and interest in their lives, and by sharing with them open and loving communication. By communicating with our youth and by encouraging them to share their heartfelt emotions and concerns, we teach them that expressing themselves is a good thing and that, even though we may not always have the answers, we encourage them to ask the questions. Our children should know, without a doubt, that they can come to us, that they can lean on us, and that they can trust us.

We must also have faith and trust in our children. Trusting our young people to do the right thing at the right time and reminding ourselves what it felt like to be their age is important for a good relationship with our children. If they have proven themselves to be trustworthy and mature in the past, we should trust them to do the same in the future, but always with the proper guidance and supervision. We build an atmosphere of trust in the family by giving our young people more and more responsibility as they grow older and by trusting them to follow through.

When parents are actively involved in their children's lives, when they offer them genuine love and encouragement, when they pray *with* them and *for* them, and when they foster an atmosphere of trust and respect in the home, they contribute to the unity of the family. Why is the unity of the family so important? 'Abdu'l-Bahá offers us these loving words, *"Note ye how easily, where unity existeth in a given family, the affairs of that family are conducted; what progress the members of that family make, how they prosper in the world. Their concerns are in order, they enjoy comfort and tranquillity, they are secure, their position is assured, they come to be envied by all. Such a family but addeth to its stature and its lasting honor, as day succeedeth day.*"[60]

There are many words of wisdom that we hope to share with our young people before they leave home and go out into the world. Some of these words of wisdom are: trust in God and accept His will; leave the world a better place than you found it; be confident that you can make a difference in the world; recognize the greatness in every human being; count your blessings; and, every day and in every way, try to exemplify Bahá'u'lláh's teachings in your lives. By sharing these words with our children, we help them to prepare for their futures. By sharing our love of the Bahá'í writings, we offer them the moral compass on which to guide their lives. And by showing them our unconditional love and support, we teach them that they are beautiful in God's sight and beautiful in ours. How great is the power of love? 'Abdu'l-Bahá writes, *"Love revealeth with unfailing and limitless power the mysteries latent in the universe."*[61]

Through their knowledge of the Bahá'í writings and through the loving guidance that they receive from their parents, our young people will meet their futures with faith and with courage. They will understand that life is not always going to be easy but that they can rely upon God to help them on their way. With goodness and with light, they will shine out like stars in the heaven of understanding. And just as stars were used to guide the ships of old at night, so will our children guide others with their beautiful light. To help them on their way, 'Abdu'l-Bahá offers these inspiring words. He writes,

Wherefore, O ye illumined youth, strive by night and by day to unravel the mysteries of the mind and spirit, and to grasp the secrets of the Day of God. Inform yourselves of the evidences that the Most Great Name hath dawned. Open your lips in praise. Adduce convincing arguments and proofs. Lead those who thirst to the fountain of life; grant ye true health to the ailing. Be ye apprentices of God; be ye physicians directed by God, and heal ye the sick among humankind. Bring those who have been excluded into the circle of intimate friends. Make the despairing to be filled with hope. Waken them that slumber; make the heedless mindful.

Such are the fruits of this earthly life. Such is the station of resplendent glory.[62]

AFTERWORD

O thou true friend! Read, in the school of God,
the lessons of the spirit, and learn from love's Teacher
the innermost truths. Seek out the secrets of Heaven,
and tell of the overflowing grace and favor of God.

—'Abdu'l-Bahá, Selections from the Writings of 'Abdu'l-Bahá

What is the legacy that we will leave behind as parents? We may never really know the full extent of our efforts or how much we may have impacted our children's lives or the lives of those around us. We may only get a glimpse of its great magnitude in the next life. But one thing is for certain—our lives affect not only our children's lives, but our children's children, and their children's children, and so on. No one knows how much we may have changed the future except for God. I think Howard Colby Ives said it best when he wrote,

> Like a pebble cast into a calm pool the ripples from that little deed spread and spread to infinity. And, as they spread, they touch the ripples from tens, scores, thousands of others' deeds, expressions, gestures, thoughts; each affected by each until one

becomes conscious of the vast responsibility each soul takes upon itself by the mere fact of acting his part, living his life through one little moment of time. He sees himself a king affecting for better or worse every soul in the world, sooner or later, by the very breath he draws, the thoughts of his inmost heart.[1]

Our children are our legacy, our unique gift that we offer to the world. Because of them, the world is changed for the better or for the worse. It will be the challenges and the difficulties that they face that will help them to determine their characters. It will be their faith and their spirits that will help them to determine their lives. By loving and guiding our children on a moment to moment basis, we help them to become the people who they are meant to be. This dream can become a reality. We can raise children who are a blessing to the earth and to all the people whom they may meet.

We are a large part of who our children will become, and they are a large part of who we will become. We should help each other, inspire each other, and support each other in this amazing endeavor called *Life*. Through the loving support of their parents and through the spiritual guidance that they receive from the Bahá'í writings, our children will grow up to be spiritual and strong. They will lead others by their examples and they will choose to follow the straight path.

Our children are our precious gifts, our treasured gems, our fragrant roses, our fruitful trees, and our heavenly stars. They may stumble, at times, only to rise up again, for they will know who they are. They are Children of the Kingdom.

GLOSSARY

'Abdu'l-Bahá. *Servant of Bahá.* Born 'Abbás Effendi on May 23, 1844, in Tehran, Iran. He was the eldest son of Bahá'u'lláh, Prophet-Founder of the Bahá'í Faith, and was chosen by Bahá'u'lláh to be His successor. He assumed the title of "'Abdu'l-Bahá" after the death of Bahá'u'lláh in 1892, and he led the Bahá'í Faith until his death in 1921. He is also referred to as the Master, the Center of the Covenant, the Mystery of God, and the Perfect Exemplar of Bahá'u'lláh's teachings.

Abhá Paradise. The next life; the spiritual realm where the soul travels after the death of the body. *Abhá* means "Most Glorious" in Arabic.

'Akká (Acre). The ancient port city in what is now Israel where Bahá'u'lláh, His family, and His companions were exiled and imprisoned by the Ottoman Empire. Bahá'u'lláh named this city "the Most Great Prison" because of its difficult living conditions and because of the suffering that went on inside its walls.

Alláh-u-Abhá. An Arabic phrase meaning "God is Most Glorious," which Bahá'ís recite ninety-five times daily. It is also used as a greeting by Bahá'ís.

Ancient Beauty. A name referring to Bahá'u'lláh.

Ayyám-i-Há. Days of Há. The Arabic letter *Há* has the numerical value of 5. These are the four days (or five days in leap year) that occur before the month of fasting. They are also known as the Intercalary Days. It is a time for charity, hospitality, gift-giving, and a time to prepare oneself spiritually for the Fast.

Báb, the. *The Gate.* The title assumed by Siyyid 'Alí-Muḥammad, Prophet-Founder of the Bábí Faith and Forerunner of Bahá'u'lláh. The Báb was born on October 20, 1819, in S̲h̲íráz, Iran, and He was a descendent of the Prophet Muḥammad. He declared His mission in 1844 and was subsequently persecuted, imprisoned, and eventually martyred in 1850.

Bábís. Followers of the Báb, many of whom lost their lives because of their Faith.

Bahá'í International Community. The international nongovernmental organization that represents over five million members of the Bahá'í Faith. The BIC seeks to promote and apply principles derived from the teachings of the Bahá'í Faith that contribute to the resolution of current challenges facing humanity.

Bahá'í World Center. The world spiritual and administrative center of the Bahá'í Faith located in Haifa and 'Akká, Israel.

Bahá'ís. Followers of Bahá'u'lláh.

Bahá'u'lláh. *The Glory of God.* Title of Mírzá Ḥusayn-'Alí, Prophet-Founder of the Bahá'í Faith. He was born on November 12, 1817, to a noble family of Núr in Tehran, Iran. He declared His mission in 1863, wrote numerous Tablets of spiritual guidance and wisdom, and ascended to the next world in 1892. He is also referred to as the Blessed Beauty, the Blessed Perfection, and the Promised One of All Ages.

Bayán. The title of the two major works of the Báb.

Blessed Beauty. A title of Bahá'u'lláh.

Covenant of Bahá'u'lláh. The divinely ordained "instrument" provided by Bahá'u'lláh to protect the unity of the Bahá'í Faith. He accomplished this by appointing His eldest son, 'Abdu'l-Bahá, as the "Center of the Covenant" and His successor. Later, 'Abdu'l-Bahá appointed his grandson, Shoghi Effendi, to be the Guardian of the Bahá'í Faith. Since the passing of Shoghi Effendi, the Bahá'í world looks to the Universal House of Justice for leadership.

Creative Word. The Writings of Bahá'u'lláh as revealed to Him by God.

Dawn-Breakers, The. The account of the early days of Bábí history written by Nabíl-i-A'ẓam, who was a Bábí. This work was later translated into English by Shoghi Effendi.

Devotional gatherings. Spiritual gatherings devoted to worshiping God and to sharing the Bahá'í Writings or other religious texts.

Dispensation. The period of time associated with each Manifestation of God.

Faizi, Abu'l Qásim. Persian Bahá'í who was chosen to be a Hand of the Cause of God by Shoghi Effendi. He was born in 1906 and died in 1980.

Fast. The nineteen days in which Bahá'ís between the ages of fifteen and seventy abstain from eating and drinking between sunrise and sunset. The month of fasting takes place from March 2nd through March 20th. It is a period of prayer, meditation, reflection, and of turning toward God.

Feast, Nineteen Day. Gatherings for Bahá'ís that take place on the first day of every Bahá'í month, each month consisting of nineteen days and bearing the name of one of the attributes of God, such as Jamál or "Beauty." The Feast is made up of three distinct parts—the devotional portion, the administrative portion, and the social portion.

Feast letter. Monthly correspondence from the National Spiritual Assembly.

Fireside. An informal meeting for the purpose of sharing the teachings of the Bahá'í Faith.

Greatest Holy Leaf. A title given to Bahíyyih K͟hánum, the daughter of Bahá'u'lláh and the sister of 'Abdu'l-Bahá.

Haifa. A seaport in northern Israel and the administrative center of the Bahá'í Faith.

Hands of the Cause of God. Individuals appointed by Bahá'u'lláh and later by Shoghi Effendi who were responsible for the protection and the promulgation of the Bahá'í Faith.

Hidden Words, The. A collection of Arabic and Persian verses revealed by Bahá'u'lláh in 1858 in Bag͟hdád as He walked on the banks of the Tigris River.

Holy Days. Special days that commemorate significant Bahá'í anniversaries. These holy days are:
    Festival of Naw-Rúz (Bahá'í New Year): March 21
    Festival of Riḍván (Declaration of Bahá'u'lláh): April 21–May 2
    Declaration of the Báb: May 23
    Ascension of Bahá'u'lláh: May 29
    Martyrdom of the Báb: July 9
    Birth of the Báb: October 20
    Birth of Bahá'u'lláh: November 12
    Day of the Covenant: November 26
    Ascension of 'Abdu'l-Bahá: November 28

Ives, Howard Colby. A Unitarian minister who met 'Abdu'l-Bahá in 1912 during his visit to North America. He subsequently became a Bahá'í and wrote the book *Portals to Freedom* to describe his experience with 'Abdu'l-Bahá. He died in 1941.

Kitáb-i-Aqdas. *The Most Holy Book (Kitáb* means "book"; *Aqdas* means "Most Holy"). The chief repository of Bahá'u'lláh's laws that was revealed in 'Akká in 1873.

Knights of Bahá'u'lláh. The title given to Bahá'ís who traveled to different parts of the world to establish the Faith of Bahá'u'lláh in regions previously uninhabited by Bahá'ís.

Laws of God. The laws revealed by the Manifestations of God. There are two types of laws—the eternal laws that are spiritual in nature and do not change, and the social laws that are given to humanity for a particular stage in human history. Some of the laws for one's personal life are daily prayer, fasting, engaging in a trade or profession, and abstaining from partisan politics. There are also prohibitions against backbiting, gambling, and the nonmedical use of alcohol or drugs.

Letters of the Living. The first eighteen people who became followers of the Báb.

Local Spiritual Assembly. The local administrative body of the Bahá'í community that consists of nine people who are elected annually by the members of the local Bahá'í community and who administer the affairs of that community.

Louis Gregory. Prominent African-American Bahá'í born in 1874 in South Carolina. He was a member of the National Spiritual Assembly of the United States and was named a Hand of the Cause of God after his death in 1951.

Martyrs. Individuals who willingly suffer death instead of renouncing their religion.

Mashriqu'l-Adhkár. An Arabic term meaning "the Dawning-place of the praise or remembrance of God." It is the name of the Bahá'í Houses of Worship throughout the world.

Master. A title of 'Abdu'l-Bahá.

Mount Carmel. The mountain referred to by Isaiah as the "mountain of the Lord." It is located in Haifa, Israel, and is also the location of the Bahá'í World Center and the Shrine of the Báb.

National Spiritual Assembly. The national administrative body of the Bahá'í Faith that is elected annually and that oversees the work of the Bahá'í Faith in its own country.

Obligatory Prayers. The three specific prayers revealed by Bahá'u'lláh to be recited daily. Bahá'ís can choose whichever one they wish—the short obligatory prayer, the medium obligatory prayer, or the long obligatory prayer.

Pilgrimage. A journey made to a shrine or holy place. Bahá'ís go on pilgrimage to Haifa and 'Akká, Israel, where the Bahá'í shrines and the administrative center of the Faith are located. Bahá'ís are encouraged to go on pilgrimage at least once in a lifetime.

Purest Branch. Title given to Mírzá Mihdí, a son of Bahá'u'lláh, who served as His Father's amanuensis. He died in 1870 after falling to his death in the Most Great Prison in 'Akká. He was twenty-two.

Queen Marie of Romania. The first monarch to embrace the teachings of the Bahá'í Faith. Marie was Queen of Romania from 1914 to 1927. She learned about the Bahá'í Faith from Martha Root.

Revelation. The Word of God as revealed through His Manifestations.

Root, Martha. An American Bahá'í who dedicated her life to teaching the Bahá'í Faith throughout the world. She was born in 1872 and died in 1939.

Rúḥíyyih Rabbani (Rúḥíyyih Khánum). Born Mary Sutherland Maxwell in 1910. She was the wife of Shoghi Effendi and served as his personal secretary. She was named a Hand of the Cause of God in 1952 and wrote *The Priceless Pearl,* a biography about the life of

Shoghi Effendi. Rúḥíyyih, which means "spiritual," was the name given to her by Shoghi Effendi on the occasion of their marriage. She died in 2000.

Sacred Word. The writings of the Báb, Bahá'u'lláh, and 'Abdu'l-Bahá, the sacred scriptures of the Bahá'í Faith.

Shoghi Effendi. The title by which Shoghi Rabbani, the eldest grandson of 'Abdu'l-Bahá, is known to Bahá'ís. (*Shoghi* means "the one who longs" and *Effendi* signifies "sir" or "master.") He was born in 'Akká in 1897 and became the Guardian of the Bahá'í Faith in 1921. He led the Faith for over thirty years until his death in 1957.

Shrines, Bahá'í. Holy sites associated with the Báb, Bahá'u'lláh, and 'Abdu'l-Bahá. The Shrine of Bahá'u'lláh, outside of 'Akká, Israel, is the holiest spot on the earth for Bahá'ís.

Síyáh-Chál. *The Black Pit.* The subterranean dungeon in Tehran in which Bahá'u'lláh was imprisoned from August through December 1852 and where He received a Revelation from God.

Sun of Reality. A name referring to God.

Sun of Truth. A name referring to God.

Ṭáhirih. *The Pure One.* A title given by the Báb to Fátimih Umm-Salamih. She was born in 1814 in Qazvin, Iran, and was the only female Letter of the Living. She was martyred in 1852 at the age of thirty-six. She is also known as Qurratu'l-'Ayn, meaning "Solace of the Eyes."

Universal House of Justice. The supreme administrative body of the Bahá'í Faith whose members are elected every five years by members of the National Spiritual Assemblies. Their headquarters are in Haifa, Israel.

NOTES

Preface

    1. ʿAbduʾl-Bahá, *Selections from the Writings of ʿAbduʾl-Bahá,* no. 12.1.

1 / The Baháʾí Writings: A Doorway to Knowledge

    1. Baháʾuʾlláh, *Gleanings from the Writings of Baháʾuʾlláh,* no. 74.1.

    2. ʿAbduʾl-Bahá, quoted in *The Importance of Deepening our Knowledge and Understanding of the Faith,* no. 68.

    3. Ives, *The Song Celestial,* Prelude.

2 / The Individual as Spiritual Being

    1. Baháʾuʾlláh, *Gleanings from the Writings of Baháʾuʾlláh,* no. 27.2.

    2. Ives, *Portals to Freedom,* p. 63.

    3. ʿAbduʾl-Bahá, *Selections from the Writings of ʿAbduʾl-Bahá,* no. 17.2–3.

3 / Marriage and Family: A Sacred Bond of Love

1. 'Abdu'l-Bahá, *Paris Talks*, no. 58.1–3.

2. Ibid., no. 58.7.

3. 'Abdu'l-Bahá, *Selections from the Writings of 'Abdu'l-Bahá*, no. 86.2.

4. Bahá'u'lláh, in *Bahá'í Prayers*, p. 118.

5. 'Abdu'l-Bahá, *Selections from the Writings of 'Abdu'l-Bahá*, no. 88.1–2.

6. Ibid., no. 12.1.

7. 'Abdu'l-Bahá, quoted in *Bahá'í Marriage and Family Life*, no. 26.

4 / Pregnancy: The Soul and the Beginning of Spiritual Education

1. Bahá'u'lláh, *Gleanings from the Writings of Bahá'u'lláh*, no. 82.1.

2. 'Abdu'l-Bahá, *Paris Talks*, no. 28.6.

3. Ibid., no. 29.13.

4. On behalf of the Universal House of Justice, in *Lights of Guidance*, no. 2120.

5. 'Abdu'l-Bahá, *Selections from the Writings of 'Abdu'l-Bahá*, no. 12.1.

6. Bahá'u'lláh, *Gleanings from the Writings of Bahá'u'lláh*, no. 82.6.

7. Bahá'u'lláh, Hidden Words, Arabic, no. 4.

5 / Infants: God's Precious Gift

1. Bahá'u'lláh, Hidden Words, Persian, no. 29.

2. Bahá'u'lláh, *Tablets of Bahá'u'lláh revealed after the Kitáb-i-Aqdas*, p. 168.

3. 'Abdu'l-Bahá, in *Bahá'í Education*, no. 42.

4. 'Abdu'l-Bahá, in *Lights of Guidance*, no. 1005.

5. Ibid., no. 998.

6. 'Abdu'l-Bahá, in *Foundations for a Spiritual Education*, p. 65.

7. 'Abdu'l-Bahá, in *Bahá'í Education*, no. 79.

8. 'Abdu'l-Bahá, *Selections from the Writings of 'Abdu'l-Bahá*, no. 113.1.

9. 'Abdu'l-Bahá, in *Foundations for a Spiritual Education*, p. 65.

10. 'Abdu'l-Bahá, in *Bahá'í Education*, no. 79.

11. Ibid., no. 78.

12. On behalf of Shoghi Effendi, in *Family Life*, no. 60.

13. On behalf of the Universal House of Justice, *Lights of Guidance*, no. 2118.

14. 'Abdu'l-Bahá, *Selections from the Writings of 'Abdu'l-Bahá*, no. 114.1.

15. Ibid., no. 96.1–2.

16. On behalf of the Universal House of Justice, in *Women*, no. 68.

17. 'Abdu'l-Bahá, *Paris Talks*, no. 1.13.

18. 'Abdu'l-Bahá, in *Bahá'í Prayers*, pp. 33–34.

6 / Little Children: Gems of Inestimable Value

1. Abu'l-Qasim Faizi, *Mr. Faizi on Education*, DVD.

2. Bahá'u'lláh, *Gleanings from the Writings of Bahá'u'lláh*, no. 122.1.

3. Ibid., no. 136.2.

4. 'Abdu'l-Bahá, *Selections from the Writings of 'Abdu'l-Bahá*, no. 115.2.

5. Ibid., no. 115.3.

6. Bahá'u'lláh, The Kitáb-i-Íqán, ¶233.

7. On behalf of Shoghi Effendi, in *The Unfolding Destiny of the British Bahá'í Community*, p. 446.

8. Ibid., p. 154.

9. 'Abdu'l-Bahá, in *Bahá'í Prayers*, p. 29.

10. 'Abdu'l-Bahá, *The Promulgation of Universal Peace*, p. 71.

11. 'Abdu'l-Bahá, *Selections from the Writings of 'Abdu'l-Bahá*, no. 74.2.

12. Universal House of Justice, in *Lights of Guidance*, no. 1365.

13. 'Abdu'l-Bahá, in ibid., no. 1828.

14. On behalf of the Universal House of Justice, in *The Compilation of Compilations*, 1:979.

15. Bahá'u'lláh, *Tablets of Bahá'u'lláh revealed after the Kitáb-i-Aqdas*, p. 88.

16. Bahá'u'lláh, *Epistle to the Son of the Wolf*, p. 50.

17. Faizi, *Mr. Faizi on Education*, DVD.

18. Ives, *Portals to Freedom*, pp. 115–17.

19. Shoghi Effendi, *God Passes By*, p. 283.

20. 'Abdu'l-Bahá, *Paris Talks*, no. 55.2.

21. 'Abdu'l-Bahá, *Selections from the Writings of 'Abdu'l-Bahá*, no. 123.2.

22. Ibid., no. 159.2.

23. 'Abdu'l-Bahá, *The Promulgation of Universal Peace*, pp. 315–16.

24. Bahá'u'lláh, *Gleanings from the Writings of Bahá'u'lláh*, no. 156.1.

25. 'Abdu'l-Bahá, *Selections from the Writings of 'Abdu'l-Bahá*, no. 1.7.

26. 'Abdu'l-Bahá, *Paris Talks*, no. 1.7.

27. 'Abdu'l-Bahá, *Selections from the Writings of 'Abdu'l-Bahá*, no. 138.4.

28. Bahá'u'lláh, *Gleanings from the Writings of Bahá'u'lláh*, no. 125.3.

29. 'Abdu'l-Bahá, *Selections from the Writings of 'Abdu'l-Bahá*, no. 138.1.

30. 'Abdu'l-Bahá, in *Bahá'í Education*, no. 79.

31. 'Abdu'l-Bahá, *Selections from the Writings of 'Abdu'l Bahá*, no. 129.4.

32. Kitáb-i-Aqdas, Notes, no. 167.

33. Bahá'u'lláh, Kitáb-i-Aqdas, ¶74.

34. Ibid., ¶151.

35. Ibid., ¶74.

36. 'Abdu'l-Bahá, *The Promulgation of Universal Peace*, p. 262.

37. 'Abdu'l-Bahá, *Selections from the Writings of 'Abdu'l-Bahá*, no. 96.1.

38. The Universal House of Justice, *Riḍván 2000 Message*, ¶25.

39. On behalf of Shoghi Effendi, in *Bahá'í Education*, no. 134.

40. 'Abdu'l-Bahá, *Selections from the Writings of 'Abdu'l-Bahá*, no. 95.2.

41. Ibid.

42. Faizi, *Mr. Faizi on Education*, DVD.

43. Ibid.

44. From a letter written on behalf of the Universal House of Justice to an individual believer, in *Guidelines for Spiritual Assemblies on Domestic Violence*, p. 22.

45. On behalf of the Universal House of Justice, in *Lights of Guidance*, no. 509.

46. On behalf of Shoghi Effendi, in ibid., no. 510.

47. Bahá'u'lláh, in *Bahá'í Education*, no. 14.

48. Faizi, *Mr. Faizi on Education*, DVD.

49. Rabbani, *The Priceless Pearl*, pp. 6–8.

50. Ibid., pp. 5–6.

51. 'Abdu'l-Bahá, *Selections from the Writings of 'Abdu'l-Bahá*, no. 106.1–2.

7 / School-Age Children: Roses of One Garden

1. 'Abdu'l-Bahá, in *Bahá'í Education*, no. 100.

2. 'Abdu'l-Bahá, *Selections from the Writings of 'Abdu'l-Bahá*, no. 95.2.

3. 'Abdu'l-Bahá, in *Bahá'í Education*, no. 78.

4. Bahá'u'lláh, in ibid., no. 20.

5. Bahá'u'lláh, Kitáb-i-Aqdas, ¶48.

6. 'Abdu'l-Bahá, *Selections from the Writings of 'Abdu'l-Bahá*, no. 101.1.

7. Kitáb-i-Aqdas, Notes, no. 76.

8. 'Abdu'l-Bahá, in *Bahá'í Education*, no. 82.

9. Bahá'u'lláh, *Epistle to the Son of the Wolf*, p. 26.

10. Bahá'u'lláh, *Tablets of Bahá'u'lláh revealed after the Kitáb-i-Aqdas*, p. 168.

11. 'Abdu'l-Bahá, *Selections of the Writings of 'Abdu'l-Bahá*, no. 110.1.

12. Ibid., no. 119.2.

13. Bahá'u'lláh, in *Bahá'í Education*, no. 20.

14. 'Abdu'l-Bahá, *Selections of the Writings of 'Abdu'l-Bahá*, no. 121.1.

15. 'Abdu'l-Bahá, *Promulgation of Universal Peace*, pp. 71–72.

16. 'Abdu'l-Bahá, *Selections from the Writings of 'Abdu'l-Bahá*, no. 72.2.

17. Bahá'u'lláh, in *Bahá'í Education*, no. 17.

18. 'Abdu'l-Bahá, in *The Importance of the Arts in Promoting the Faith*, no. 13.

19. 'Abdu'l-Bahá, *Paris Talks*, no. 55.1.

20. 'Abdu'l-Bahá, *Promulgation of Universal Peace*, p. 261.

21. 'Abdu'l-Bahá, *Selections from the Writings of 'Abdu'l-Bahá*, no. 102.3.

22. Bahá'u'lláh, *Gleanings from the Writings of Bahá'u'lláh*, no. 99.4.

23. Ibid., no. 148.1.

24. Bahá'u'lláh, *Tablets of Bahá'u'lláh revealed after the Kitáb-i-Aqdas*, p. 156.

25. Bahá'u'lláh, *Gleanings from the Writings of Bahá'u'lláh*, no. 153.7.

26. Bahá'u'lláh, Kitáb-i-Aqdas, ¶182.

27. Bahá'u'lláh, *Gleanings from the Writings of Bahá'u'lláh*, no. 82.5.

28. Ibid., no. 124.2.

29. 'Abdu'l-Bahá, in *Bahá'í Education*, no. 73.

30. 'Abdu'l-Bahá, *Selections from Writings of 'Abdu'l-Bahá*, no. 12.1.

31. 'Abdu'l-Bahá, *Promulgation of Universal Peace*, p. 359.

32. 'Abdu'l-Bahá, *Selections from the Writings of 'Abdu'l-Bahá*, no. 12.1.

33. Bahá'u'lláh, Hidden Words, Arabic, no. 5.

34. Bahá'u'lláh, *Gleanings from the Writings of Bahá'u'lláh*, no. 153.5.

35. Bahá'u'lláh, *Epistle to the Son of the Wolf*, p. 83.

36. Ives, *Portals to Freedom*, pp. 36–38.

37. Ibid., pp. 39–40.

38. Ibid., pp. 48–49.

39. 'Abdu'l-Bahá, *Selections from the Writings of 'Abdu'l-Bahá*, no. 172.1.

40. The Báb, *Selections from the Writings of the Báb*, 3:2:4.

41. Honnold, Annamarie (ed.), in *Vignettes from the Life of 'Abdu'l-Bahá*, pp. 148–49.

42. Bahá'u'lláh, in *The Compilation of Compilations*, 1:5.

43. Bahá'u'lláh, Kitáb-i-Aqdas, ¶138.

44. Ibid., Questions and Answers, no. 68.

45. On behalf of Shoghi Effendi, in *Bahá'í Education*, no. 130.

46. Bahá'u'lláh, in *Bahá'í Education*, no. 23.

47. Bahá'u'lláh, Kitáb-i-Aqdas, ¶150

48. Rabbani, *The Priceless Pearl*, pp. 8–9.

49. 'Abdu'l-Bahá, *Selections from the Writings of 'Abdu'l-Bahá*, no. 108.2.

50. On behalf of Shoghi Effendi, in *Bahá'í Education*, no. 126.

51. Bahá'u'lláh, *Gleanings from the Writings of Bahá'u'lláh*, no. 136.6.

52. 'Abdu'l-Bahá, *The Promulgation of Universal Peace*, p. 534.

53. 'Abdu'l-Bahá, *The Secret of Divine Civilization*, p. 98.

54. 'Abdu'l-Bahá, in *Women*, no. 41.

55. 'Abdu'l-Bahá, *Selections from the Writings of 'Abdu'l-Bahá*, no. 110.2.

56. Ibid., no. 123.1–3.

57. 'Abdu'l-Bahá, in *Bahá'í Education*, no. 92.

58. 'Abdu'l-Bahá, *Selections from the Writings of 'Abdu'l-Bahá*, no. 108.1.

59. 'Abdu'l-Bahá, in *Bahá'í Education*, no. 96.

60. 'Abdu'l-Bahá, *Selections from the Writings of 'Abdu'l-Bahá*, no. 111.7.

61. Ibid., no. 111.1.

62. Ibid., no. 2.16.

63. Bahá'u'lláh, *Tablets of Bahá'u'lláh revealed after the Kitáb-i-Aqdas*, p. 36.

64. 'Abdu'l-Bahá, in *Bahá'í Education*, no. 42.

65. Ibid.

66. 'Abdu'l-Bahá, *Selections from the Writings of 'Abdu'l-Bahá*, no. 110.3.

67. Bahá'u'lláh, Kitáb-i-Aqdas, ¶46.

68. Kitáb-i-Aqdas, Notes, no. 74.

69. 'Abdu'l-Bahá, in *The Importance of the Arts in Promoting the Faith*, no. 24.

70. 'Abdu'l-Bahá, *Selections from the Writings of 'Abdu'l-Bahá*, no. 129.4.

71. Morrison, *To Move the World*, p. 94.

72. Ibid., p. 319.

73. Bahá'u'lláh, *Gleanings from the Writings of Bahá'u'lláh*, no. 110.1.

74. Ibid., no. 43.5.

75. 'Abdu'l-Bahá, *The Promulgation of Universal Peace*, p. 128.

76. On behalf of Shoghi Effendi, in *Bahá'í Marriage and Family Life*, no. 214.

77. 'Abdu'l-Bahá, in *Family Life*, no. 9.

78. 'Abdu'l-Bahá, *Selections from the Writings of 'Abdu'l-Bahá*, no. 137.2.

79. Ibid., no. 1.1.

80. 'Abdu'l-Bahá, in *Bahá'í Education*, no. 94.

81. 'Abdu'l-Bahá, in *Developing Distinctive Bahá'í Communities*, no. 13.2.

82. On behalf of the Universal House of Justice, in *The Compilation of Compilations*, no. 981.

83. 'Abdu'l-Bahá, *Selections from the Writings of 'Abdu'l-Bahá*, no. 124.1.

84. Bahá'u'lláh, in *Bahá'í Education*, no. 14.

85. On behalf of Shoghi Effendi, in *Bahá'í Education*, no. 130.

86. 'Abdu'l-Bahá, *Selections from the Writings of 'Abdu'l-Bahá*, no. 111.4.

87. Ibid., no. 110.1.

88. Ibid.

89. 'Abdu'l-Bahá, in *Bahá'í Education*, no. 64.

90. Bahá'u'lláh, in ibid., no. 28.

91. On behalf of Shoghi Effendi, in *Developing Distinctive Bahá'í Communities*, 11.19–20.

92. Bahá'u'lláh, in *Family Life*, no. 44.

93. Bahá'u'lláh, Kitáb-i-Aqdas, Questions and Answers, no. 106.

94. 'Abdu'l-Bahá, in *Family Life*, no. 55.

95. 'Abdu'l-Bahá, in *Bahá'í Marriage and Family Life*, no. 177.

96. Bahá'u'lláh, in *Lights of Guidance*, no. 768.

97. 'Abdu'l-Bahá, quoted in *Portals to Freedom*, p. 52.

98. Ives, *Portals to Freedom*, pp. 194–95.

99. 'Abdu'l-Bahá, *The Promulgation of Universal Peace*, p. 304.

100. 'Abdu'l-Bahá, *Selections from the Writings of 'Abdu'l-Bahá*, no. 103.1.

8 / Junior Youth: Fruitful Trees

1. Bahá'u'lláh, *Gleanings from the Writings of Bahá'u'lláh*, no. 129.2.

2. 'Abdu'l-Baha, *Paris Talks*, no. 54.13.

3. Ibid, no. 54.11.

4. Bahá'u'lláh, *Gleanings from the Writings of Bahá'u'lláh*, no. 79.1.

5. 'Abdu'l-Bahá, *Paris Talks*, no. 54.9.

6. On behalf of Shoghi Effendi, in *Lights of Guidance*, no. 1483.

7. 'Abdu'l-Baha, *Paris Talks*, no. 26.7.

8. On behalf of Shoghi Effendi, in *Lights of Guidance*, no. 1914.

9. On behalf of Shoghi Effendi, in *Bahá'í Education*, no. 148.

10. Bahá'u'lláh, in *The Importance of Deepening our Knowledge and Understanding of the Faith*, no. 6.

11. 'Abdu'l-Bahá, *Selections from the Writings of 'Abdu'l-Bahá*, no. 1.7.

12. Ibid.

13. Bahá'u'lláh, *Gleanings from the Writings of Bahá'u'lláh*, no. 117.1.

14. 'Abdu'l-Baha, quoted in Lady Blomfield, *The Chosen Highway*, p. 167.

15. 'Abdu'l-Baha, *The Secret of Divine Civilization*, p. 59.

16. Bahá'u'lláh, Kitáb-i-Aqdas, Notes, no. 175.

17. Bahá'u'lláh, *Gleanings from the Writings of Bahá'u'lláh*, no. 164.2.

18. Bahá'u'lláh, Hidden Words, Persian, no. 3.

19. Ibid., from the Persian, no. 56.

20. Táhirih, quoted in Shoghi Effendi, *God Passes By*, p. 75.

21. Root, *Táhirih the Pure*, p. 88.

22. 'Abdu'l-Bahá, quoted in H. M. Balyuzi, *'Abdu'l-Bahá*, p. 9.

23. 'Abdu'l-Baha, *Selections from the Writings of 'Abdu'l-Baha*, no. 100.2.

24. Bahá'u'lláh, in *Bahá'í Education*, no. 12.

25. 'Abdu'l-Bahá, in *Bahá'í Prayers*, pp. 30–31.

26. Bahá'u'lláh, Hidden Words, Arabic, no. 48.

27. Bahá'u'lláh, *Gleanings from the Writings of Bahá'u'lláh*, no. 123.4.

28. 'Abdu'l-Bahá, *Paris Talks*, no. 23.7.

29. Bahá'u'lláh, Hidden Words, Arabic, no. 22.

30. Bahá'u'lláh, *Epistle to the Son of the Wolf*, pp. 25–26.

31. A letter written on behalf of Shoghi Effendi, quoted in *Foundations for a Spiritual Education*, p. 29.

32. Bahá'u'lláh, *Tablets of Bahá'u'lláh revealed after the Kitáb-i-Aqdas,* p. 168.

33. 'Abdu'l-Bahá, *Selections from the Writings of 'Abdu'l-Bahá,* no. 122.1.

9 / Youth: Stars of the Heaven of Understanding

1. On behalf of the Universal House of Justice, in *Messages from the Universal House of Justice, 1963–86,* no. 426.2.

2. Bahá'u'lláh, Kitáb-i-Aqdas, ¶10.

3. On behalf of Shoghi Effendi, in *Lights of Guidance,* no. 1523.

4. 'Abdu'l-Bahá, in *The Importance of Obligatory Prayer and Fasting,* p. 14.

5. Ibid., pp. 17–18.

6. Bahá'u'lláh, Kitáb-i-Aqdas, ¶18.

7. Shoghi Effendi, *Principles of Bahá'í Administration,* p. 9.

8. Bahá'u'lláh, in *The Importance of Obligatory Prayer and Fasting,* p. 2.

9. Ibid.

10. Ibid., pp. 2–3.

11. 'Abdu'l-Bahá, *Selections from the Writings of 'Abdu'l-Bahá,* no. 107.1.

12. Ibid., no. 174.3.

13. Bahá'u'lláh, *Gleanings from the Writings of Bahá'u'lláh,* no. 2.1.

14. Ibid., no. 155.5.

15. 'Abdu'l-Bahá, *The Promulgation of Universal Peace,* p. 647.

16. Ibid., p. 409.

17. Ibid.

18. Bahá'u'lláh, *Epistle to the Son of the Wolf,* p. 9.

19. 'Abdu'l-Bahá, *The Promulgation of Universal Peace,* p. 415.

20. Bahá'u'lláh, Hidden Words, Arabic, no. 2.

21. Bahá'u'lláh, *Tablets of Bahá'u'lláh revealed after the Kitáb-i-Aqdas,* p. 51.

22. Bahá'u'lláh, *Gleanings from the Writings of Bahá'u'lláh,* no. 77.1.

23. Bahá'u'lláh, in *Bahá'í Education,* no. 26.

24. 'Abdu'l-Bahá, in ibid., no. 79.

25. 'Abdu'l-Bahá, in *Lights of Guidance,* no. 717.

26. 'Abdu'l-Bahá, in *Bahá'í Education,* no. 79.

27. Bahá'u'lláh, *Tablets of Bahá'u'lláh revealed after the Kitáb-i-Aqdas,* p. 26.

28. On behalf of the Universal House of Justice, in *Lights of Guidance,* no. 2154.

29. 'Abdu'l-Bahá, in *Bahá'í Education,* no. 30.

30. Bahá'u'lláh, in *Youth,* no. 1.

31. 'Abdu'l-Bahá, *The Promulgation of Universal Peace,* p. 10.

32. The Universal House of Justice, in *Lights of Guidance,* no. 2134.

33. Bahá'u'lláh, Hidden Words, Persian, no. 36.

34. Bahá'u'lláh, *Gleanings from the Writings of Bahá'u'lláh,* no. 5.3.

35. On behalf of Shoghi Effendi, in *Youth,* no. 26.

36. M. R. Garis, *Martha Root: Lioness at the Threshold,* p. 240.

37. Marie, Queen of Rumania, in the *Toronto Daily Star,* 4 May 1926, reprinted in *The Bahá'í World,* Vol. II, p. 174.

38. Gail, Marzieh, in Martha Root, *Táhirih the Pure*, pp. xvii–xviii.

39. Martha Root, quoted in M. R. Garis, *Martha Root: Lioness at the Threshold*, p. 485.

40. Shoghi Effendi, *God Passes By*, p. 386.

41. Bahá'u'lláh, Kitáb-i-Aqdas, ¶117.

42. 'Abdu'l-Bahá, *The Promulgation of Universal Peace*, p. 265.

43. Ibid, pp. 265–66.

44. On behalf of Shoghi Effendi, in *Lights of Guidance*, no. 2131.

45. Bahá'u'lláh, Hidden Words, Persian, no. 76.

46. Bahá'u'lláh, *Gleanings from the Writings of Bahá'u'lláh*, no. 90.1.

47. Ibid., no. 96.3.

48. 'Abdu'l-Bahá, *Selections from the Writings of 'Abdu'l-Bahá*, no. 86.1.

49. Ibid., no. 84.2–4.

50. On behalf of the Universal House of Justice, in *Lights of Guidance*, no. 1216.

51. The Universal House of Justice, in *Developing Distinctive Bahá'í Communities*, no. 17.3.

52. 'Abdu'l-Bahá, *Paris Talks*, no. 50.8.

53. 'Abdu'l-Bahá, in *Bahá'í Education*, no. 85.

54. 'Abdu'l-Bahá, *Selections from the Writings of 'Abdu'l-Bahá*, no. 85.1.

55. Bahá'u'lláh, Kitáb-i-Aqdas, ¶65.

56. Shoghi Effendi, in Bahá'u'lláh, Kitáb-i-Aqdas, Notes, no. 92.

57. The Universal House of Justice, in *Lights of Guidance*, no. 1237.

58. 'Abdu'l-Bahá, *Selections from the Writings of 'Abdu'l-Bahá*, no. 92.1–3.

59. 'Abdu'l-Bahá, *The Promulgation of Universal Peace*, pp. 232–33.

60. 'Abdu'l-Bahá, *Selections from the Writings of 'Abdu'l-Bahá*, no. 221.9.

61. Ibid., no. 12.1.

62. 'Abdu'l-Bahá, in *Bahá'í Education*, no. 106.

Afterword

1. Ives, *Portals to Freedom*, p. 39.

BIBLIOGRAPHY

Writings of Bahá'u'lláh

Epistle to the Son of the Wolf. Translated by Shoghi Effendi. Wilmette, IL: Bahá'í Publishing Trust, 1988.

Gleanings from the Writings of Bahá'u'lláh. Translated by Shoghi Effendi. 1st ps ed. Wilmette, IL: Bahá'í Publishing, 2005.

The Hidden Words. Translated by Shoghi Effendi et al. Wilmette, IL: Bahá'í Publishing, 2002.

The Kitáb-i-Aqdas: The Most Holy Book. 1st ps ed. Wilmette, IL: Bahá'í Publishing Trust, 1993.

The Kitáb-i-Íqán: The Book of Certitude. Translated by Shoghi Effendi. New ps ed. Wilmette, IL: Bahá'í Publishing, 2003.

Tablets of Bahá'u'lláh revealed after the Kitáb-i-Aqdas. Compiled by the Research Department of the Universal House of Justice. Translated by Habib Taherzadeh et al. 1st ps ed. Wilmette, IL: Bahá'í Publishing Trust, 1988.

245

Writings of the Báb

Selections from the Writings of the Báb. Compiled by the Research Department of the Universal House of Justice. Translated by Habib Taherzadeh et al. 1ˢᵗ ps ed. Wilmette, IL: Bahá'í Publishing Trust, 2006.

Writings of 'Abdu'l-Bahá

Paris Talks: Addresses Given by 'Abdu'l-Bahá in 1911. Wilmette, IL: Bahá'í Publishing, 2006.

The Promulgation of Universal Peace: Talks Delivered by 'Abdu'l-Bahá during His Visit to the United States and Canada in 1912. Compiled by Howard MacNutt. New ed. Wilmette, IL: Bahá'í Publishing Trust, 2007.

The Secret of Divine Civilization. Translated by Marzieh Gail and Ali-Kuli Khan, 1ˢᵗ ps ed. Wilmette, IL: Bahá'í Publishing, 2007.

Selections from the Writings of 'Abdu'l-Bahá. Compiled by the Research Department of the Universal House of Justice. Translated by a Committee at the Bahá'í World Center and Marzieh Gail. Wilmette, IL: Bahá'í Publishing, 2010.

Writings of Shoghi Effendi

God Passes By. Introduction by George Townshend. Wilmette, IL: Bahá'í Publishing Trust, 2004.

Principles of Bahá'í Administration: A Compilation. London: Bahá'í Publishing Trust, 1976.

The Unfolding Destiny of the British Bahá'í Community: The Messages from the Guardian of the Bahá'í Faith to the Bahá'ís of the British Isles. London: Bahá'í Publishing Trust, 1981.

Writings of the Universal House of Justice

Messages from the Universal House of Justice, 1963–1986: The Third Epoch of the Formative Age. Compiled by Geoffry W. Marks. Wilmette, IL: Bahá' í Publishing Trust, 1996.

Riḍván 2000 Message. Bahá'í World Centre.

Compilations of Bahá'í Writings

Bahá'í Education: A compilation of extracts from the Bahá'í Writings. Compiled by the Research Department of the Universal House of Justice. 2nd revised ed. London: The Bahá'í Publishing Trust, 1998.

Bahá'í Marriage and Family Life: Selections from the Writings of the Bahá'í Faith. Wilmette, IL: Bahá'í Publishing Trust, 1997.

Bahá'í Prayers: A Selection of Prayers revealed by Bahá'u'lláh, the Báb, and 'Abdu'l-Bahá. Wilmette, IL: Bahá'í Publishing Trust, 2002.

The Compilation of Compilations: Prepared by the Universal House of Justice, 1963–1990. 2 vols. Australia: Bahá'í Publications Australia, 1991.

Family Life. Compiled by the Research Department of the Universal House of Justice. Wilmette, IL: Bahá'í Publishing Trust, 2008.

Foundations for a Spiritual Education: Research of the Bahá'í Writings. Prepared by the National Bahá'í Education Task Force. Wilmette, IL: National Spiritual Assembly of the Bahá'ís of the United States.

The Importance of the Arts in Promoting the Faith: A Compilation. Ontario, Canada: Bahá'í Canada Publications in cooperation with Palabra Publications, 1999.

The Importance of Deepening our Knowledge and Understanding of the Faith: Extracts from the Writings of Bahá'u'lláh, 'Abdu'l-Bahá and Shoghi Effendi. Compiled by the Universal House of Justice. Ontario, Canada: The National Spiritual Assembly of Canada, 1983.

The Importance of Obligatory Prayer and Fasting: Selection of Extracts and Prayers from the Bahá'í Writings. Compiled by the Research Department of the Universal House of Justice. NSW, Australia: Bahá'í Publications Australia, 2001.

Lights of Guidance: A Bahá'í Reference File. Compiled by Helen Bassett Hornby. New Delhi: Bahá'í Publishing Trust, 2004.

Spiritual Foundations: Prayer, Meditation, and the Devotional Attitude. Extracts from the Writings of Bahá'u'lláh, 'Abdu'l-Bahá, and Shoghi Effendi. Compiled by the Research Department of the Universal House of Justice. Wilmette, IL: Bahá'í Publishing Trust, 1980.

Women: Extracts from the Writings of Bahá'u'lláh, 'Abdu'l-Bahá, Shoghi Effendi and the Universal House of Justice. Compiled by the Research Department of the Universal House of Justice. Thornhill, Ontario: Bahá'í Canada Publications, 1986.

Youth: Extracts from the Writings of Bahá'u'lláh, 'Abdu'l-Bahá and Shoghi Effendi. Compiled by the Research Department of the Universal House of Justice. Mona Vale NSW, Australia: Bahá'í Publications Australia, 1995.

Other Sources

Balyuzi, H. M. *'Abdu'l-Bahá: The Centre of the Covenant*. Oxford: George Ronald, 1992.

Blomfield, Lady (Sitárih K͟hánum). *The Chosen Highway*. Wilmette, IL: Bahá'í Publishing Trust, n.d.; repr. 1975.

Faizi, Abu'l-Qasim. *Mr. Faizi on Education*. Unedited DVD. U. S. Bahá'í Media Services.

Garis, M. R. *Martha Root: Lioness at the Threshold*. Wilmette, IL: Bahá'í Publishing Trust, 1983.

Honnold, Annamarie, ed. *Vignettes from the Life of 'Abdu'l-Bahá*. Oxford: George Ronald, 1997.

Ives, Howard Colby. *Portals to Freedom*. Oxford: George Ronald, 1983.

————. *The Song Celestial*. Copyright September 1938 by Howard Colby Ives. Republished by Erich P. Reich Enterprises, Oregon.

Morrison, Gayle. *To Move The World: Louis G. Gregory and the Advancement of Racial Unity in America*. Wilmette, IL: Bahá'í Publishing Trust, 1982.

On behalf of the National Spiritual Assembly of the Bahá'ís of the United States and Canada, *The Bahá'í World, Vol. II, 1926–1928*, 1928.

On behalf of the Office of Assembly Development. *Developing Distinctive Bahá'í Communities: Guidelines for Spiritual Assemblies*. Evanston, IL: National Spiritual Assembly of the Bahá'ís of the United States, 2007.

Rabbani, Rúḥíyyih. *The Priceless Pearl*. London: Bahá'í Publishing Trust, 1969.

Root, Martha. *Táhirih The Pure*. Los Angeles: Kalimát Press, 1981.

AND THE BAHÁ'Í FAITH

Bahá'í Publishing produces books based on the teachings of the Bahá'í Faith. Founded over 160 years ago, the Bahá'í Faith has spread to some 235 nations and territories and is now accepted by more than five million people. The word "Bahá'í" means "follower of Bahá'u'lláh." Bahá'u'lláh, the founder of the Bahá'í Faith, asserted that He is the Messenger of God for all of humanity in this day. The cornerstone of His teachings is the establishment of the spiritual unity of humankind, which will be achieved by personal transformation and the application of clearly identified spiritual principles. Bahá'ís also believe that there is but one religion and that all the Messengers of God—among them Abraham, Zoroaster, Moses, Krishna, Buddha, Jesus, and Muḥammad—have progressively revealed its nature. Together, the world's great religions are expressions of a single, unfolding divine plan. Human beings, not God's Messengers, are the source of religious divisions, prejudices, and hatreds.

The Bahá'í Faith is not a sect or denomination of another religion, nor is it a cult or a social movement. Rather, it is a globally recognized independent world religion founded on new books of scripture revealed by Bahá'u'lláh.

Bahá'í Publishing is an imprint of the National Spiritual Assembly of the Bahá'ís of the United States.

For more information about the Bahá'í Faith,
or to contact Bahá'ís near you,
visit http://www.bahai.us/
or call
1-800-22-unite

OTHER BOOKS AVAILABLE FROM

BAHÁ'Í PUBLISHING

THE FACE OF GOD AMONG US
How the Creator Educates Humanity
John S. Hatcher
$17.00 U.S. / $19.00 CAN
Trade Paper
ISBN 978-1-931847-70-4

The Face of God among Us is an examination of religious history that aims to find out exactly who the founders of the great religions of the past were, and what their role has been in the development of human society. Author John Hatcher looks at the lives and stations of the Prophets of the past—Buddha, Krishna, Zoroaster, Moses, Jesus Christ, Muḥammad, the Báb, and Bahá'u'lláh—and asks: Who exactly were these exalted beings? Were they ordinary humans, temporarily inspired by God? Are they God incarnate, as some believe? Or are they a different category of being all together? In the course of his investigation, Hatcher uncovers a pattern in religious history that seems to hold the answers to all these questions. In doing so, he offers a new insight into the method by which the Creator educates humankind, and provides us with a fascinating perspective about our existence on this planet.

ILLUMINE MY BEING
Bahá'í Prayers and Meditations for Health
Bahá'u'lláh and 'Abdu'l-Bahá
$14.00 U.S. / $16.00 CAN
Trade Paper
ISBN 978-1-931847-69-8

Illumine My Being is a collection of prayers and meditations from Bahá'í scripture that are intended to provide spiritual healing for the individual during times of crises. Many of these prayers ask God for the healing of the individual as well as the community, the nation, and the world. These extracts from the sacred writings explain how individual healing can be achieved through one's relationship with God, and they also elaborate on the nature of spiritual healing and how the healing of the entire human race can be achieved. Healing has always been an essential component of religion, and these prayers and meditations are meant to provide comfort, hope, and reassurance to anyone during these troubled times.

LONGING

Stories of Racial Healing

Phyllis A. Unterschuetz and Eugene F. Unterschuetz

$15.00 U.S. / $17.00 CAN

Trade Paper

ISBN 978-1-931847-68-1

Longing: Stories of Racial Healing is a collection of true stories from the journey of one white couple toward understanding their hidden fears, prejudices, and ultimate connection to African Americans. It contains matter-of-fact statements about the fear and suspicion that both African Americans and whites still harbor toward one another, and it describes how these barriers can, with the right amount of effort, be overcome. As diversity trainers, the authors have traveled throughout the United States, speaking about racial unity and the oneness of humanity. They describe uncomfortable and embarrassing situations, examine mistakes and unconscious assumptions, and share what they have learned about being white. Their stories contain revelations from black friends and strangers who taught them to see beyond superficial theories and to confront the attitudes that have shaped how Americans think about race. But above all, their stories speak about the longing they discovered everywhere they traveled—a longing to connect and to heal from the racial separation that has so deeply wounded this country.

SELECTIONS FROM THE WRITINGS OF 'ABDU'L-BAHÁ
'Abdu'l-Bahá
$14.00 U.S. / $16.00 CAN
Trade Paper
ISBN 978-1-931847-74-2

Selections from the Writings of 'Abdu'l-Bahá is a compilation of correspondence and written works of one of the central figures of the Bahá'í Faith. 'Abdu'l-Bahá, meaning "Servant of the Glory," is the title assumed by 'Abbás Effendi (1844–1921)—the eldest son and appointed successor of Bahá'u'lláh, the Prophet and Founder of the Bahá'í Faith. After his father's passing in 1892, 'Abdu'l-Bahá assumed leadership of the worldwide Bahá'í community until the time of his own passing in 1921. During that time he corresponded with Bahá'ís all over the world, providing them with an abundance of practical and spiritual guidance. The works collected here cover a wide range of topics including physical and spiritual health, death and the afterlife, the spiritual reality of humankind, the oneness of humanity, and the elimination of prejudice. The wisdom imparted in this volume remains as timeless and relevant today as when it was first committed to paper.